ADVANCE PRAISE

"Ka-Ching! They say the CFO role should pay for itself, and this is a book that will pay for itself many times over. Pam Prior's Chapter 4 "signature exercise" alone will save business owners many thousands of dollars. Whether you're looking to add a bookkeeper, part-time CFO or full-time CFO, this book is an eye-opening must-read."

–Kevin Kruse, *New York Times* bestselling author and Inc 500 Entrepreneur

"As a CEO, having an executive team that provides substantive feedback is essential, especially in areas of finance and operations. Having been lucky enough to work directly with Pam over the years through complex corporate turnaround projects, I know first-hand that making accounting and finance a vital partner in the leadership of a company is essential. The blueprint provided in this book in a fun, readable format is easily tailored for implementation in any small business."

–Amelia Warner, CEO, Global Specimen Solutions

T0098568

"Pam Prior was not my first CFO, but she was the very best – and I'm still learning from her as I read her new book, *Your First CFO*. As might be expected with Pam's stellar accounting credentials and past experience, she is unparalleled in her mastery of financial and accounting management. Her aptitude, however, goes far beyond her "mere" academic genius: she has strong leadership skills and exceptional organizational competencies. She is a remarkable individual, and this outstanding book provides great insight into her blueprint for success. In *Your First CFO*, Pam does an incredible job of distilling important principles into quick nuggets of information that are adaptable to businesses of all sizes. I'm glad to have this book in my arsenal of business literature and I recommend it to all."

–Joe Chandler, **President**, **SPI International Transportation**

"Finally! A financial management book that I can recommend to my clients without hesitation. Pam Prior's *Your First CFO* tackles one of the most beguiling tasks for entrepreneurs – how to successfully manage business financials *and* the people who provide them. Like Nathalie, the compilation client in *Your First CFO*, many owners intuitively know every detail of their business *except* how the financial statements work together and create a roadmap for improvement and success. Well-written and easy to understand, this book gives any CEO the tools needed to make smart decisions, whether they are hiring a part-time bookkeeper or a full-time CFO."

–Gina Catalano, Business Coach and best-selling author of *Tandem Leadership*: *How Your #2 Can Make You #1*

YOUR FIRST CFO

YOUR FIRST STEP

YOUR FIRST CFO

*The Accounting Cure
for Small Business Owners*

PAM PRIOR

NEW YORK

LONDON • NASHVILLE • MELBOURNE • VANCOUVER

YOUR FIRST CFO
The Accounting Cure for Small Business Owners

Published in New York, New York, by Morgan James Publishing in partnership with Difference Press. Morgan James is a trademark of Morgan James, LLC. www.MorganJamesPublishing.com

The Morgan James Speakers Group can bring authors to your live event. For more information or to book an event visit The Morgan James Speakers Group at www.TheMorganJamesSpeakersGroup.com.

ISBN 9781683505556 paperback
ISBN 9781683505563 eBook
Library of Congress Control Number: 2017906382

Cover Design by:
Rachel Lopez
www.r2cdesign.com

Interior Design by:
Chris Treccani
www.3dogcreative.net

In an effort to support local communities, raise awareness and funds, Morgan James Publishing donates a percentage of all book sales for the life of each book to Habitat for Humanity Peninsula and Greater Williamsburg.

Get involved today! Visit
www.MorganJamesBuilds.com

Dedicated to Sharon, Steve, Mike, Ray, Bill, and Dick – the amazing finance leaders at DuPont Pharmaceuticals who taught me the most important lesson:

The *how* is as important as the *what*.

And to Dr. Amelia Warner who lit the way.

And to Deb and Lindsey – my reasons.

TABLE OF CONTENTS

Introduction   *xv*

Chapter 1   **Draw Your Business: Business Mapping**   **1**
                 Draw Your Business – Q & A   4

Chapter 2   **Notice the Connections: Linking Net**
                 Income and Cash   **11**
                 Cash Flow Statement Analysis   17
                 Profit and Loss Statement Analysis   26
                 The Big Picture: Trends   32

Chapter 3   **Look Ahead: Forecasting**   **39**
                 Forecasting Basics   42
                 13-Week Cash Flow Forecast   54

Chapter 4	**Meet Your Cash: Controls Over Cash**	**61**
	For One Month, Sign Every Check	63
	Balance the Checkbook	65
Chapter 5	**Gain Insight: More about Key Performance Indicators**	**69**
	Contribution Margin Percentage	77
	Days Sales Outstanding (DSO)	78
	Days Payables Outstanding (DPO)	79
	Inventory Conversion Ratio	80
	Other KPIs	81
Chapter 6	**Build Your Team: Finance and Accounting Roles**	**87**
	Financial Roles	95
Chapter 7	**Pick Your CFO: The Range of CFO Choices**	**105**
	Full-Time CFO	106
	Interim and Part-Time CFOs	108
Further Resources		*115*
Acknowledgments		*117*

About the Author 119

Thank You 121

INTRODUCTION

It had been the longest of days for Nathalie, CEO of RunTrue Productions. The only thought rolling through her head on the drive home (in rush-hour traffic, up I-95 out of Philadelphia, in a car that hadn't been cleaned out for months), was, *I'm going to kill my bookkeeper!* Nathalie had a critical meeting at the bank the next day, and Frank (her bookkeeper) had just told her that the monthly RunTrue financials weren't going to be ready until Friday.

Two days late.

Again.

Nathalie had been leaving messages for Frank daily, reiterating how this month had to be different and he had to get her the financials on time. She normally didn't get upset at the unpredictable timing of her financial reports – which always came way too late to be useful (even if they'd made sense to her). But *this* month, Frank had promised to meet his contracted commitment of getting them to her within two weeks after the end of the month. The bank was insisting on seeing last month's numbers before committing to the new loan Nathalie needed for the business.

And, speaking of the new loan, how on earth could the business be running out of cash within the next two months? It had been showing a profit on the Profit and Loss Statements Frank eventually sent to her, and yet the balance in the cash account had been dropping like a stone. *It makes no sense*, Nathalie thought as she drove. *I'm going to kill my bookkeeper. No worries, though. I'll just hire another one next week.* There seemed to be thousands of bookkeepers out there, all of them promising the world.

Nathalie had worked her way through three bookkeepers in two years without 1) gaining any real understanding of her company's financial position, 2) ever getting a month-end report on time, or 3) being able to remotely relate the things that showed up on the report to the way she ran her business.

It struck Nathalie that she even though she was a business owner and entrepreneur, she had been running her business without financial information that was 1) reliable, 2) timely, or 3) relevant.

RunTrue was about to launch a whole new product line that would likely double revenues, and yet she wasn't sure whether it would lead to more cash in the bank. That reminded her of a podcast she'd listened to (during yet another commute, a few days ago), by somebody she respected, who'd said, "What gets measured gets done." As Nathalie took Exit 46 off the highway to start on the last three miles to her house in Bucks County, PA, she thought *I'm not measuring anything.*

How could she know where the business had been, where it was, and, most importantly, what was ahead, without measuring? How could she evaluate decisions about clients, employees, service-providers, leased space, or growth plans, if she didn't have a clear and reliable way to measure how and what she and the business were doing?

The only things she knew for sure as she pulled into the driveway of her Toll Brothers McMansion, and before she shifted into parent mode for the night (she was convinced that business owners never got to focus 100% on their families) were that 1) the car needed to be cleaned out tonight, or she was going to dump every last thing in it into the garbage at 5 a.m. the next morning before she left for work; and 2) she needed to do something radically different to get a handle on her business finances.

She got out of the car and opened the door from the garage into the utility room and, right there, before she went inside, she made a commitment to herself that something had to change, and it had to change tomorrow. Even so, she knew she wasn't going to sleep well tonight.

The next morning, Nathalie was very pleasantly surprised to find that her car had already been cleaned out. Her husband, Dave, had recognized her frustration level the night before and simply taken care of it for her. He knew well that her concerns about the car actually had nothing to do with the car. That was one of the reasons Nathalie loved him – for his ability to find ways to show his unwavering support and faith in her during her day-to-day whirlwind. She was self-aware enough to know that her stress over the car was a thin veil on the mess surrounding the business finances, and her inability see through it to the clarity she needed.

Who knew? Maybe the clean car was an omen of cleaner things to come for her financials.

She set out to meet the banker in Center City, without the financial statements, but, at the very least, she could quiz the banker on some of the finer points of his decision-making process for evaluating her loan request.

During the meeting (*after* she'd spilled her Starbucks coffee on her white blouse), Nathalie asked questions. The banker answered. But his answers took the form of more questions and paralyzed Nathalie because she couldn't answer them in return.

How long had she been in business? What were the company's assets? How much had she invested? Was the company paying dividends? Was any of her current debt secured? Would she sign a personal guaranty? How did she measure business performance? What was her liquidity ratio? What was her debt to equity ratio? What was her profit margin? How about her operating margin?

The banker asked for "the trailing twelve months of all three key financial statements." He wanted Nathalie's perspective on the company's financial trends. How did those look related to the forecast? What was her DSO? What was her DPO? What was her cost of customer acquisition? Did she have any sole-source providers? What was her EBITDA? Did her operating cash flow cover investment needs? Were her ratios improving or deteriorating?

Stop!! Stop!! Nathalie wanted to scream.

All his questions hit her like an avalanche, crushing her. Only two years ago, she'd moved from a financial system that consisted of a shoebox of receipts to agreeing to pay $25,000 a year for an outsourced bookkeeper. And yet she *still* didn't know *any* of the answers to the key questions the banker was asking. And – what the heck? – now she was being asked to put her family's home on the line by signing a personal guaranty? *Good Lord, my business has been profitable!* Nathalie wanted to scream at the banker. Her biggest frustration was that she couldn't explain why her business needed a loan in the first place.

She held her tongue, thanked the banker, said she'd get back to him shortly, walked outside to the street, and called me.

I'd met Nathalie that morning at the Starbucks she'd visited before her bank meeting. She was clearly distressed after spilling her coffee, so I'd offered her a Tide-to-Go stick for the stain on her blouse and we chatted long enough for me to realize that she needed to decompress, so I had given her my number. Thus began our journey together.

* * *

Nathalie is an amalgamation of solopreneurs, entrepreneurs, small- to mid-size business owners, and CEOs I've worked with and that span every sector of our economy (from manufacturing to services to distribution and retail). Nathalie is by no means alone, and her journey to turn finances from foe into friend is one I have enjoyed helping many business owners and CEOs take.

If you developed sweaty palms while reading and relating to Nathalie's story, take three to four deep breaths, relax, and read on.

In the coming chapters, I'll cover how to find answers to every single question Nathalie was asked about her business and her finances. Those answers are attainable, and they are enlightening. I will also help you understand that you already possess all the intellect and energy required to get a handle on your finances. By the time you finish this book, you'll know how easy your finances can be to manage, and how powerfully and positively they can enlighten your business decisions.

Drawing on my extensive background in the accounting and finance fields, and on my experiences working in many industries, I lay out a path to bring you clarity and to free you from nightmares like Nathalie's.

What we're going to talk about in this book is likely going to be different from any conversation you've had to date with your bookkeeper or accountant. The powerful concepts in this small book are presented in business persons' English, just like I presented them to Nathalie when we met to talk about her finances. I will walk you through Nathalie's transformation from finance victim to confident, calm commander of her company's financial story.

You've arrived at a level of success in your business where the accounting is something you are ready to delegate. Accounting and dealing with financial reporting don't need to already be crystal clear to you in order to apply the concepts covered in this book. In fact, the job of this book is to *remove* you from the mundane, frustrating, time-consuming pieces of the accounting and reporting process, so you can focus instead on enjoying your reliable and timely monthly financial reports and put them to valuable use leading your organization.

This may be a big ask, but do yourself a favor and read on from a place of faith that you can get to that place of enjoyment with such a dry topic. Bookkeeping, accounting, and financial reporting can be and will become your allies, your friends in the foxhole, and anything but the enemy that they may currently seem to be.

Get ready to minimize your involvement in your accounting and financial reporting process, while maximizing the value you extract from it.

* * *

Let's start with a little background about accounting and finance.

No matter what anyone tells you to the contrary, and no matter how complicated anyone tries to make the terminology and the process sound, you really can become the master of every single question that arose during Nathalie's story. It is 100% achievable for you as a business owner.

The things you will discover as you follow this roadmap will lead you to the same confidence level Nathalie now has. This book will lead you to:

- Understand how your *business levers* or *controls* are reflected in your financials, and what actions you can take to increase or decrease profit and cash flow.
- Understand the elusive connection between the profit you see on your Profit and Loss Statement and the cash balance in your bank.
- Understand each of the three major financial statements that you need to run your business.
- Have a business leader's conceptual understanding of how the key pieces of your financial statements tie together.
- Know that the most important financial measures are those that inform your management of your business.
- Discover how to make sure that your financial statements reflect your business as you want it to be reflected.
- Extract the real value from your financials by turning them into a spotlight on the future and a way to evaluate all your significant business decisions.

- Develop an understanding of key accounting and finance roles and responsibilities to help you delegate, and to ensure that you transform from frustrated to enlightened business owner.

That may seem like a tall order for a single book. Dealing with accounting and financials is a process that has long been the bane of the business-owner's existence (and has certainly been the butt of many a good joke), but there is a method you can learn that is business-owner-friendly, focused on adding value, and worthy of your investment to learn it.

Your financials should be your allies. You deserve to crave and enjoy seeing them each month. You deserve to be able to interpret, with very little effort, what they mean and how they relate to your wonderful plans for your business. You deserve to have processes in place that support you and your business, and people in place who understand your business and are fully aligned with its strategy. All of these are attainable, no matter how big or small your business is or how new your business is.

It's lonely enough at the top. You have enormous responsibilities, you rise to constant challenges, you discover new opportunities, you provide exceptional value to your customers, and you care deeply about the people for whom you are providing a paycheck. That all combines to cause significant pressure, day in and day out. This book promises that the financial reporting piece – this one very tangible, yet crucial, aspect of your leadership – can be resolved to the point of being your ally, and not just another pressure point.

You already know how important this is. You know that your bankers and investors need you to be in command of the finance and accounting process. You know that your clients expect your business to thrive, and that your suppliers and employees expect to be paid.

Yet, up until now, a true grasp of your financial reports has been elusive, pushed to the back of the pile. You have probably placed a disproportionate amount of reliance upon the people in these two roles: a bookkeeper, whose job it is to create a monthly report for you; and an accountant, whose job it is to file your tax returns for you. Both serve key roles, but neither is focused on what *you* need to *run* the business. There is nothing in the middle tying together the distinct goals of the bookkeeper and tax accountant unless you, with this book, step into that gap.

There is *so* much value to be extracted from placing your attention in the gap between those two roles – from bookkeeper to you to the accountant. There's so much value there that will put you at ease, that will enlighten your decision-making and that will help you predict cash needs with much more accuracy.

I will show you how to set up a system to establish a repeatable, reliable, timely, transparent, and accurate financial reporting process focused on *you*. It only needs to be set up once, and in the right way. Then your role becomes that of interpreter, leader, guide, decision maker, and strategist. This is as it should be.

Read these coming chapters and then come back to them as you need to for reference while you set up your process. The chapters show how to move from a financial process that approximates facing backward in a sinking rowboat approaching an iceberg, to one that's more like facing forward in a sailboat, where slight movements on the rudder steer you away from harm and into the future you envision for the business you love.

The tools and concepts needed to make this happen already exist. The people you need already exist. You don't have to invent them (or avoid them). By using the principles in this book, you will get those people and concepts working *for* you. You will feel the relief of having timely, reliable, and relevant financial reports that you can trust, and insights that propel you forward, so you aren't held hostage to bookkeeping traditions, lofty accounting terminology, and not knowing what to ask. You are not alone at the beginning of this journey, and you will feel a new level of relief at the end of it.

* * *

There is a story that has played itself out repeatedly in so many of our lives. The *anticipation* of something we know we *should* do, but which seems like it will be an awful drain on our energy, our emotions, our time, and our productivity. So we keep putting it off, but all that does is lengthen that awful period of negative anticipation. Does this tend to be your pattern around your company's finances?

Even when the ultimate action we take does turn out to be painful, the longer we take to get around to *doing* it, the longer the pain lasts. The sooner we start the actual *doing*, the sooner the agony ends. In the case of getting your financial reporting system in order, even if the set-up involves some learning, the resulting (smoother) process will not be nearly as painful as the anticipation and procrastination were.

The roadmap in this book has been developed throughout my 25-year career, and includes my experiences:

- Reviving distressed companies
- Laying the groundwork for growing companies
- Supporting pre-funding start-ups
- Thriving in a Fortune 100 career

- Working with the federal agencies that established internal control standards for small companies
- Leading successful information systems implementations
- Integrating and consolidating multiple international subsidiaries
- Forming, aligning, and leading teams
- Making mistakes and learning from them
- Exceeding expectations
- Leading regulatory financial reporting in public companies
- Creating and participating in investment road shows
- Securing financing
- Participating in board meetings
- Leading due diligence and post-acquisition integrations
- Learning and growing in various roles, including:
  - Mail room clerk
  - Accountant
  - Team Leader
  - Accounting supervisor
  - Accounting manager (for domestic and international companies)
  - Controller (domestic and international)
  - Chief financial officer (domestic and international)
  - Chief operating officer

In short, *I know my stuff.* Early in my professional career, I benefited from working with an outstanding finance leadership team. I will always be indebted to that team of leaders for teaching me that *how* we do things is just as important as *what* we do. I learned, and have carried with me, 1) that the results of my career are *my own* responsibility; 2) that I am never a victim of circumstances; and 3) to always to give back. If I'm any kind of author, the spirit of those leaders to whom I'm indebted will be reflected throughout this book as clearly as they are in the dedication.

Accounting is complex. It is a hard-earned credential to be a CPA, and bookkeeping is a learned skill. I could share about all of that – but not in this book. Without minimizing the complexity and knowledge with which bookkeepers and accountants operate, *this* book shows you how to *run your business.*

As a business leader, you need to operate from a place where you fully trust that the complexities of accounting and bookkeeping are capably managed by your experts, and that the system is set up so that you can extract *only* and *exactly* the information you need to run your business.

There are so many under-served business owners and CEOs in small- to mid-sized businesses. Like you may be, they are drowning in accounting details that are presented in formats that don't align with how they think about their businesses. As an entrepreneur, you deserve to know what questions to ask, to know how you get the answers, and to know what services to expect from your accounting and finance teams.

Whether your financial team is in house or outsourced, it is their responsibility to align with *your* business, not the other way around.

Read on, and learn how to make it so.

CHAPTER 1

Draw Your Business: Business Mapping

The most important reason for you to read this book is to realize that, to be a successful business leader, you need to come to terms with accounting.

Ouch.

My goal is to make that journey as painless and valuable as possible, and with one clear takeaway in mind:

Your business accounting only has value to you if it is aligned with your business model.

That sounds so simple. And yet, when I met Nathalie, she was caught in a quagmire of reports that didn't have value for her. She, like so many others, reviewed monthly reports that had been set up using generic templates, and that didn't reflect the business that she was running, day in and day out.

To turn the corner and step into a better system, one that worked for Nathalie, the accounting team first needed to understand Nathalie's business. So, together, we walked through a series of questions that translated Nathalie's business from the crystal-clear vision in her head into the language required by Frank (her bookkeeper) to support that vision. That exercise laid the groundwork for Frank to start creating reports and metrics that *made sense to Nathalie* and that logically and obviously reflected her own concept of her business model.

Your first step, like Nathalie's, is to create a clear description, in English, of your business the way *you* see it. To do this well, you're going to need some uninterrupted time. And, since this description will become the foundation on which you build your financial confidence, get a babysitter for the kids, close the door (or head to your favorite off-site hideaway), turn off the phones, and promise yourself to spend fifty uninterrupted minutes to answer the questions (coming up soon, in the next section).

Fifty minutes for this is just right. If you finish early, go back over your answers and see if you've missed anything. If it takes longer than 50 minutes, you're getting too detailed (remember the 80/20 rule: 80% of the value is in 20% of the effort; so take the high, 30,000-foot perspective for this exercise as you look at your vision for your business.) You don't need to be perfect here; you only need to capture the outline of your business essentials, as *you* see them.

If you have trusted advisors, check in and ask them the same questions, and listen to their answers carefully. Your own filter may be misleading you about your vision. If you have a mastermind or peer group you can brainstorm with, pull them together and run them through this exercise, as well. If you have a trusted leadership team, get those team members' perspectives.

As you go through this exercise and answer the questions, there is a ground rule (and it may surprise you):

Define your business *without* looking at your current financial reports or asking your accounting team what is possible.

This blank-page approach will define your business as *you* see it, not necessarily as your current accounting and reporting reflects it.

Now, don't panic. I am not proposing the start of a major project to overhaul everything about your accounting and reporting systems. Alignment to create a system that really works for you may only require a few tweaks. That will be more likely if you are completely transparent about how *you* see your business, and about what information you'd like to have at your fingertips to manage it. For now, don't worry about how we will accomplish that vision, just grab a notebook, or open a new computer document, and let's go.

Draw Your Business – Q & A

1. Overview
   a. What are the things you purchase and/or pay for to run your business (where does your cash go)?
      i. Supplies
      ii. Services
      iii. Employees
      iv. Consultants
      v. Materials
      vi. Other
   b. What are the services or products you create or modify to provide to your clients (what do your clients pay you for)?

c. What do you do to transform and create the services or products that you provide to your clients (or, what is your "special sauce")?

d. What is your core expertise? In other words, why are you in business, and what are the things that only you can do, that can't be outsourced? Advice: be very selective with your answer; there should only be one or two things, at most.

e. What makes your business better than anyone else's?

f. List your competitors. What makes them strong competitors?

g. What environmental and economic factors affect your ability to do business?

2. Categories

a. Do you have different clusters of clients that group together in your mind to form categories that you would like to track?

b. Do you have different clusters of products or services that group together in your mind to form categories that you would like to track?

c. Do you operate in different geographical regions that you would like to track individually?

      d.   Are there any other characteristics or dimensions of your business model that you would like to differentiate and track?

3. Processes
    a. How are the things that you purchase and/or pay for delivered into your possession? Is the delivery process different for any of the categories identified in the previous section?
    b. How do you deliver your products or services to your clients? Is that process different for any of the categories identified in the previous section?
    c. What is the value you add to your products before you send them to or provide them to your clients? Is the added value different for any of the categories identified in the previous section?
    d. What machines, materials, and/or people are involved in creating the products or services for your client? Are they different for any of the categories identified in the previous section?
    e. What machines, supplies, people, and expenses are not specifically involved in creating the products or services that you sell?

4. Outside Factors
   a. What is the composition of your customer base? Advice: Take an 80/20 look at your customers. Who provides 80% of your customer base?
   b. Do you have any suppliers who are at risk, or who are the only suppliers for key products or services you need?
   c. Under what regulatory restrictions and requirements do you operate?
   d. Who owns you?
      i. How much have they invested?
      ii. How long have they been invested?
      iii. What are their expectations of the business? Short-term? Long-term?
   e. Who has lent you money? *Advice: This doesn't include the normal invoicing from your suppliers; only large loans or lines of credit.*
      i. How much do you owe them?
      ii. How are you paying them back?
      iii. What's the timing on paying them back?
      iv. What is the cost (interest charge)?

5. Context
    a. What are the three biggest questions or challenges you face in your business right now?
    b. If you could wave a wand, what information would you want for being able to make good decisions for each of the time periods below?
        i. Daily
        ii. Weekly
        iii. Monthly
        iv. Quarterly
        v. Annually

* * *

Welcome back. And congratulations! That was a huge first step toward gaining the control you need to make financial decisions that are in line with your vision. In addition, the information you have pulled together defines the structure that your bookkeeper can use to set up your accounting system to reflect the business as you've defined it. To put it in bookkeeper language, it is the structure for your chart of accounts and dimensional reporting.

**Make your financials work for you, not the
other way around.**

It is likely that, as you move through the rest of this book, the answer to that last question you answered – What information do you need to make good decisions? – will expand and pivot. That is good news, and so stay open to it happening.

You won't ever have *all* the answers. Business is dynamic.

The process we are developing here for you reflects the dynamic reality of business. Despite what you may have heard, accounting and reporting can, and should, be equally as dynamic as your business. Flexibility in your accounting process allows you to be more flexible in the running of your business.

Next, we'll demystify some important business accounting concepts and reports.

CHAPTER 2

Notice the Connections: Linking Net Income and Cash

There are two crucial financial statements that tie together through very basic math to create an integrated view of business performance. The most familiar to many business owners is the Profit and Loss Statement, which you may already rely on to track your net income. Contrary to popular belief, the second crucial statement is not the Balance Sheet. It is the Cash Flow Statement.

The importance of the Cash Flow Statement is often overlooked, sometimes because of its apparent disconnection to the Profit and Loss Statement, which enjoys so much popularity.

There is a clear connection between Net Income and Cash Flow that requires only a little addition and subtraction to see.

When I walked into her office for our appointment, on the Tuesday morning after our first call, Nathalie was pacing back and forth along the row of windows in her office, animatedly talking on the phone. She signaled me to come in and sit down and then put her hand over the mouthpiece and said, "Just a minute. I'm on the phone with my banker."

"Tim," Nathalie said into the phone, "I don't care what the reports say. I *know* my company is worth more than that. Also, we should definitely have the cash needed to make this purchase. I'm in this business every single day, and I know how well we're doing."

She paused while Tim talked.

"*No*, I don't have any reporting that shows what I know. I just *know* with every fiber of my being that we are *making* money, not losing it." Nathalie dug through a pile of papers on her desk and accidentally knocked her coffee cup off the edge of her desk with her elbow. She put her iPhone on the desk and tapped the speaker button.

I went to get something to clean up the spill.

When I came back into Nathalie's office with some paper towels, Nathalie had raised her voice. "No, I don't have that documented! My bookkeeper can barely get my expense reports into the system." She went back to pacing. "I'm telling you what I *know*. That's all I can do right now. You need to trust me. One, I've built this business to the size that it is; two, we're still growing; and, three, I *know* we're making money."

There was a long silence as Tim was speaking.

Nathalie sank into her chair with a long exhale. "No," she said softly, "I can't explain why our cash balance is decreasing so rapidly."

As Nathalie uttered that last sentence, I could feel the energy drain out of her and, in turn, out of the space around her. Normally a magnetic and energetic person, Nathalie suddenly looked deflated and exhausted, clearly frustrated at her inability to answer key questions about her business.

In that moment of frustration, her sigh echoed the unanswered question of way too many business leaders: *If things are going so well, why is the cash balance decreasing?*

There are logical reasons that cash *can* decrease in a profitable business.

She said goodbye to Tim, hung up the phone, and looked at me. "I can't believe that something so simple can seem so complicated," she said.

I knew that the data she needed was available – it just wasn't getting through the system translated in a way that could answer her most important questions. Luckily, Nathalie had taken time during the previous week to complete the Draw Your Business questionnaire, so we were fast off the starter blocks to get things fixed.

I opened my mouth to get us started, but Nathalie picked up the phone suddenly. Before I could stop her to let her know that she was closer to having the answers than she thought she was, she'd pressed a button on the phone. Apparently, the bookkeeper was on speed dial. And Nathalie was on a mission.

"Frank," Nathalie said, with urgency in her voice. "I need you to tell me why our cash and our net profit aren't in sync. Something's wrong with the books. Something's wrong with the way you're keeping track of things." She paused for him to respond.

"No Frank, I don't want a bank reconciliation. And I don't want to sit with you to learn the chart of accounts. I just want an answer to my question," Nathalie said.

She didn't get one.

When she hung up the phone, Nathalie looked at me with complete exasperation and said, "Now you can see why this stuff drives me crazy. There is no way we're going to get our hands on this information in time for me to react well to this opportunity I have."

I smiled, because I knew some things she didn't yet. "Here's a new coffee," I said, passing the mug to her.

She took a sip and looked at me with doubt and resignation. "I know you've said this is fixable, but I'm not convinced."

The great thing about financial systems is that they definitely are *fixable*.

I wanted to get her some instant relief, so I said, "If you give me your Income Statement and Balance Sheet from the last three months, in whatever shape they're in, I think we can get our hands on some quick answers. Then we can breathe and get things set up better to deal with these kinds of issues much less painfully in the future."

"But I don't have any time to spend on this today," Nathalie said.

"I know," I said. "I'll tell you what. Why don't you give me the reports and I'll go calculate the numbers, for now? Then I'll set it up so that you can quickly do the same thing anytime you need to in the future."

When she gave me the reports, I saw that Frank had been sending her only the Profit and Loss Statement and the Balance Sheet each month. Those were only two of the three key financial statements she needed. She was missing the most important one: the Cash Flow Statement.

The Cash Flow Statement should always be delivered with the monthly reports from your bookkeeper.

"Just to give you some immediate hope," I told Nathalie, "when you have a Cash Flow Statement included with your monthly reports, answers like the one you're looking for today will pop right out at you whenever you need them. The Cash Flow Statement is the bridge that connects everything together," I said.

"Well, okay, if you think we can get there," Nathalie said, with some skepticism. But I thought I sensed a tiny, though well-buried, return of confidence in her tone. I took her reports and headed off.

As I pointed out to Nathalie that day, although we were going to focus only on the Cash Flow Statement and P&L (Profit & Loss Statement) immediately, the Balance Sheet was an equally important part of the package. However, for purposes of gaining cash flow clarity, the relevant Balance Sheet information is addressed inside the Cash Flow Statement analysis.

Cash Flow Statement Analysis

The Cash Flow Statement is the bridge between net income and your bank balance. Net income is usually the first component of cash flow, and there are also a few other components that are added and subtracted, and that affect your bank balance, but have nothing to do with your net income. Let's take a closer look.

Cash Flow Impacts

It helps to know more about the math behind the cash deterioration issue Nathalie was facing.

The problem Nathalie wrestled with was that the net income number she saw on the Profit and Loss Statement (also known as the P&L, or the Income Statement) every month kept rising.

But every time she checked the bank balance, it was decreasing. What was happening there?

Differences between the net income you see on your P&L and changes in your bank account balance are caused (primarily) by these five typical business realities:

- You've *earned* cash from operations (so it shows on the P&L), but it's not in your bank account yet because customers haven't paid you yet (this is a change in accounts receivable)
- You've *committed* to spending cash on operations, but you haven't written the check yet; or you have, but the vendor hasn't cashed it yet (this is a change in accounts payable)
- You've *spent* cash to buy materials for operations that you haven't used yet (this is a change in inventory)
- You've *borrowed* or *paid back* cash to lenders or owners (this is a change in loans or equity)
- You've *spent* cash to buy property and equipment (this is a change in fixed assets)

The Cash Flow Statement that Nathalie hadn't been getting each month would have confirmed her gut instinct that she *should* have been making money, and show her exactly why that money wasn't showing up in the bank balance.

When Nathalie and I talked about this, she realized that her gut understanding of her business already took into consideration the last two items in the list above: She knew how much money she'd borrowed, paid back, put into the business herself, or used to buy furniture and computers.

What she was missing were the first three business considerations listed above – accounts receivable, accounts payable, and inventory. Those three contribute to what's called *operating cash flow*, which is the cash required to run normal business operations.

Operating cash flow is the cash required to run normal business operations.

To clarify the impact of normal business operations on the bank balance, let's look at the three components of operating cash flow – accounts receivable, accounts payable, and inventory – one at a time.

Accounts Receivable

Accounts receivable includes cash that's been earned (so it shows up on the P&L as sales), but it hasn't quite arrived in the bank account yet. In RunTrue's case, when we took a quick look at Nathalie's top 10 customers, we learned that two of them were taking 60 days to pay their invoices instead of the 30 days that were expected by Nathalie's company.

Also, confirming Nathalie's gut instinct, we discovered that sales were increasing drastically (a good thing), but that the growth was using even more cash. Without a Cash Flow Statement, Nathalie couldn't see that. The business was having to spend money to fulfill higher and higher levels of sales, but wasn't collecting for those sales until 30 to 60 days after the sale.

Growing your business, even without adding any expenses, eats up cash initially.

Later, after the new sales level becomes more established, more cash will flow in than flows out, but, in the beginning, growth is a cash drain. A Cash Flow Statement would have shown Nathalie what was happening around accounts receivable.

Accounts Payable

Accounts payable includes cash that your business has promised to pay, but that hasn't quite yet been disbursed. In Nathalie's company, as it turned out, a friendly competition was brewing between two well-intentioned accounts payable team members, to see who could pay their invoices most quickly. Because of that, invoices that didn't *require* payment for 30 days were actually *being* paid almost immediately upon receipt.

With a Cash Flow Statement in hand, and the application of some simple math, Nathalie would have been alerted to the accounts payable situation.

Inventory

A company's inventory is a form of cash that's hiding on the shelves. In RunTrue, the purchasing group was buying bulk inventory to get a great discount; but, because of buying such high volumes, there was a lot of inventory that stayed on the shelves for up to a full year at a time – and it was already paid for.

Nathalie wouldn't necessarily have known about this or have been able to make different decisions about inventory purchasing unless she received regular Cash Flow Statements.

Putting It All Together

The status of accounts receivable, accounts payable, and inventory explained the very large difference between RunTrue's net income, which was $3 million for the year, and the balance on the bank statements, which had decreased by $2 million since the beginning of the year, due to these factors:

- Slow collections (Accounts Receivable)
- Growth (Accounts Receivable)
- Quick vendor payment (Accounts Payable)
- Inventory discounts (Inventory)

The good news for Nathalie was that the drivers for each of those situations were very easily identified and adjusted for. Then, with the right process and reporting in place, they could be monitored from month to month. With new clarity, Nathalie called Frank and told him that he would need to start providing her with the Cash Flow Statement each month.

With the Cash Flow Statement in hand, we used simple math (addition and subtraction), as shown below, to discover the cause of the deteriorating bank balance. I showed Nathalie the following formula, starting with the net income figure on the P&L and ending with the period's change in the bank balance:

- + $3,000,000 – positive net income (from the P&L)
- - $3,250,000 – increase in accounts receivable, primarily from cash tied up in accounts receivable because of customers paying late and because of growth in sales
- - $250,000 – decrease in accounts payable, primarily from cash hurried out the door to suppliers, because of the competition between accounts payable team members
- - $1,500,000 – increase in inventory, from cash used to build up inventory for growth and to obtain bulk discounts from suppliers, resulting in a larger inventory on hand
- = - $2,000,000 – overall *decrease* in the bank balance during a year when the company was growing, and had earned $3,000,000 in net income

Implementing Change

As Nathalie and I discussed the Cash Flow Statement, she expressed her relief at finally being able to clearly see what had been driving the disconnect between her *perception* of cash flow and the *reality* of it. Yes, she would need to adjust some things, but at least the situation made sense to her. More importantly, she knew the specific actions she needed to take to recover control.

Nathalie needed to address these issues:

- **Accounts Receivable.** Check to see if the slow-paying customers were in financial distress, if their late payments were only oversights on their part, or if the billing was incorrect and thus slowing down processing on the customers' side.
- **Accounts Payable.** Commend the accounts payable clerks for their passion in setting up the "Who can clear their desk the fastest?" competition, but change the rules of the game, to incentivize a different behavior.
- **Inventory.** Help an operations team member calculate the correct volume cut-off for inventory discounts for materials purchases. In RunTrue's case, very good net income decisions made by the team members were causing negative cash flow pressures. They needed to find a better balancing point between the opposing business needs of inventory stock and cash flow.

At that point, Nathalie was eager to act on what she'd learned.

One of the slow-paying customers was a friend of Nathalie's, so she decided to call and get that cleared up quickly. When she did, she found out that her friend's company had changed their accounting system and, sure enough, they had set up the wrong payment terms for Nathalie's invoices. Her friend assured Nathalie that a check would arrive to Nathalie in two days to resolve that gap. That phone call, therefore, accelerated RunTrue's receipt of $750,000 in cash.

Nathalie knew she had to drive different behaviors from the accounts payable team members. She quickly set up a new reward system for that team that incentivized them to pay suppliers on the exact dates the bills were due, and not before. That change would slow down the exit of cash from the business by about $100,000.

To resolve the inventory overload, Nathalie decided to offer a clearance sale to her customers. She would still make more than had been spent on the inventory, and the sale would clear the shelves down to only the inventory needed to support actual production. That action pulled in an additional $1,500,000 in cash during the sale, because Nathalie stipulated that sale items required cash payment within 5 days.

In total, the effects of those three changes would make the company's bank balance $2,350,000 higher at the end of *the current month* – even without including positive cash flows from normal business operations.

Nathalie and I wrapped up our meeting, and she asked how soon we should meet again. She knew talking about the P&L was next, and she was feeling hopeful by then, so she wanted to keep up the momentum we had created.

Profit and Loss Statement Analysis

The second statement worth spending just a little bit of time with each month is the Profit and Loss Statement, the P&L. Nathalie wanted to do this next, because she was concerned about her net income. When we lined up the previous six months of P&L reports in chronological order on the conference table in her office, she pointed out that her net income as a percentage of sales had been getting smaller and smaller, but she couldn't quite figure out why or what to do to fix it.

The solution was buried in the details supporting the P&L. Let's take a look.

Net Income Impacts

RunTrue's P&L was particularly frustrating because Nathalie wanted to own a business that had at least a 15% return on sales. The term *return on sales* refers to the net income expressed as a percentage of sales. A 15% return on sales meant that Nathalie wanted the net income after all of the business expenses were deducted from sales, to be at least 15% of sales. She'd investigated her competitors and learned that, on average, they were reaching that 15% goal.

When Nathalie had asked Frank (repeatedly) why RunTrue's return was so low, all he'd told her was that expenses were high. But then if she asked him about the details behind an expense item, she got immediately frustrated, because her questions *always* revealed misclassified expenses.

No wonder she'd been shoving the P&L reports in a drawer each month! She simply hadn't had time to sort out the same or similar issues, month after month. Every month, she'd try to understand the P&L, maybe go head-to-head with Frank, and not feel like she was getting anywhere. After she'd locked that drawer, she'd inevitably sigh, and think to herself, *I wish there was even one thing that I didn't have to figure out for myself about this business.*

Then on she went, for yet another month, running her business by instinct. And she couldn't help but worry. What if her instincts were off some months? What if her instincts took too long to notice a problem?

We met over lunch at a cafe to talk about the P&L situation. It was then that Nathalie shared her concerns with me about that drawerful of P&Ls being a constant reminder that she could be missing something important.

To begin helping Nathalie regain a feeling of control, I started by asking her how she conceptualized the profitability of her business. Her response was quick. "Well, that's obvious, isn't it? Profitability is revenue minus expenses."

After taking my first bite of turkey and cheese wrap, I said, "Okay, let's talk about that for a minute. Let's talk about the Draw Your Business survey you did a few weeks ago. Tell me, how many different things does your business sell?"

"Four," she replied.

"What's the range of their pieces?"

"We have a line that's a $1,000 product, another line that's a $15,000 product, and then, on the higher end, two product lines that are $50,000 and $125,000, respectively." She responded confidently. She knew those numbers cold, as she did every other statistic she controlled.

"And what costs go with each of those product lines?"

There her confidence faltered. "Well," Nathalie said. "I don't really know that. Frank can't provide that level of detail."

"We need to help him be able to do that, so that you can understand the profitability of each business line."

I was stating the obvious, and I knew Nathalie already knew that, but I wanted to make sure we were on the same page.

"Right now, your expenses are going into one big bucket and your bookkeeper is not able to tell you about the profitability of your individual products or how they fit into your picture of the business."

"Hmm," said Nathalie. "I see that. I mean, I know *instinctively* that $125,000 revenue for the large machine is wonderful, but, in reality, if we look at the details, it could very well be costing us $130,000 to produce it. And, with the $1,000 parts, I feel sure they cost us only $5 to produce and ship, and that is a *huge* margin, but I can't *see* it on the P&L, so I can't verify it. I'm still only guessing."

Implementing Change

Our next order of business was for Nathalie to take advantage of the flexibility in her bookkeeping package.

> **The bookkeeper's role includes properly categorizing revenues and expenses into the lines of business that make sense to *you*.**

There were two things Frank needed in order to upgrade the bookkeeping process to provide the missing information.

The first was to use the business model information Nathalie and I had gathered in our initial meeting; the second was to enlist the cooperation of Nathalie's own team.

For example, when Frank got a receipt or an invoice from Nathalie's office it needed to clearly indicate which line of business it applied to.

I wanted to make the concept clear to Nathalie. "That's going to take a little bit more from you and your staff, up front, with the documentation you give Frank; but the concept of *garbage in, garbage out* applies here. However, if you guys do your piece properly and Frank and I structure the way he sets up QuickBooks so that it's based on your business vision, then you'll be able to see profitability by product lines on your P&L Statement, and that will make more sense to you."

The concept of *garbage in, garbage out* affects your P&L because every member of your team feeds data into the bookkeeping system, so every member of your team has a responsibility to make sure you don't see *garbage out* on the P&L.

Nathalie's smile confirmed that she understood the importance of her own role in the soon-to-be improved process.

But we weren't finished. Since I had her attention, I continued. "There's another problem buried in here, too, Nathalie. I heard you say you had to keep asking Frank to recategorize expenses every month, because nothing ever shows up in the right place. Let's address that directly. One of the things I suggest you do right away is grab the most recent three P&Ls and take half an hour to go through them and make a list of every single thing that is in the wrong place. Using that one list, Frank can get things categorized properly, and he can capture the process in clearly documented procedures."

Nathalie was up for it, and since she had those P&Ls with her and our appointment was scheduled for another 45 minutes, we did it right then.

When we'd finished, I grabbed the list, which I later delivered to Frank, so that he would know how to categorize each document (invoices, receipts, etc.) that he received from the team. If he were to get a new document that wasn't covered by Nathalie's list, he would also know who on Nathalie's team to call for advice.

That afternoon, Nathalie met with the whole team to lay out the plan and to reiterate the importance of their participation in the reporting process.

With those new instructions delivered to Frank and the team, Nathalie was actively revising her systems. This brings to mind another saying: *Fix it once.* When you find a mistake, a problem, or a misclassification, in the bookkeeping, it's useful to require your team to get it fixed at the source, so that the

owner of the system becomes responsible for future, similar
transactions.

> **Fix problems at the source – usually at the
> beginning of a process – so that you're not
> constantly chasing the same symptoms.**

So far in this chapter, we've set up the following reporting
systems for Nathalie:

- A Cash Flow Statement that clearly outlines the
  difference between net income and cash
- A P&L with four different lines of business, for easy
  profitability assessments
- A P&L with expenses classified the way Nathalie wants
  them to be classified

The Big Picture: Trends

There was one more thing Nathalie needed from Frank
each month that would allow her to fully address the issues
she'd grappled with on the morning she'd paced while on the

phone with her banker. That was to look at the trends in her business financials.

When Nathalie *did* look at the financial statements, she usually laid out five or six months of reports on the conference table or on her desk, like we had just recently. We'd had to look back and forth between them to try to grasp the ongoing story of her business, according to the numbers.

She wanted and needed to be able to see that her accounts receivable balance was going up over time, month after month. She needed to see *changes* in profitability for each line of business *as the year progressed*. And she needed to see if her overall expenses were increasing or decreasing *over time*, and in what areas. But all she saw when she looked at the reports were numbers that didn't seem to relate to each other.

A single point of data is useless; trends and comparisons give data context and make it meaningful.

Implementing Change

If Nathalie had a clear way to see the trends in her business numbers, then all the issues that she hadn't been able to explain

– and many of the questions that Tim, her banker, had asked her – would make more sense. She would have been alerted to issues needing her attention if she could have done even a brief monthly review of properly set-up financial statements.

For a quick fix, and to get the ball rolling on getting trends data to Nathalie, I asked Frank to begin providing her with key financial statements (Cash Flow Statement, Balance Sheet, and P&L) that included columns with data for each of the previous twelve months (this option is already available in most accounting software; if not, it can be easily created in Excel). With that small change, Nathalie would be able to quickly spot issues and opportunities in each of her monthly reports.

To raise the level of service Nathalie receives around financial reporting, I suggested that she hire an accountant to review the statements each month and provide her with an executive summary of key trends. Nathalie would set a threshold for changes that required explanation, and the accountant would do the research when anything exceeded those variances.

For example, she could tell the accountant that if office supply costs increased by more than 5% for more than two months in a row, she would need an explanation. The accountant would write out an explanation and include it with the reports, so it would be there when Nathalie first saw the reports. Having that system set up would allow her to use the reports to proceed directly to decision-making, rather than first needing to investigate every oddity herself.

A few small changes in your financial reporting system can shift your focus from details to decision-making.

* * *

What we've covered so far is that there are three financial statements to regularly review:

- Profit and Loss Statement
- Balance Sheet
- Cash Flow Statement

The two that provide the most immediate value are the P&L and the Cash Flow Statement. You probably already receive a monthly P&L, but the Cash Flow Statement may be a report you've never received.

If you do only one thing because of reading this book, I recommend that it be to start receiving and reviewing a monthly Cash Flow Statement.

**Require your bookkeeper to provide you with a Cash Flow
Statement on a monthly basis.**

All three of those financial statements can and should be
aligned with how *you* look at your business. Properly setting
up even the simplest of bookkeeping tools can provide the
information you need to make decisions based on your business
finances.

In Nathalie's case, for added clarity, I arranged the data
in her reports according to RunTrue's four product lines, so
that she could see their individual profitability. Also, we used
her Draw Your Business questionnaire to make sure expense
reporting was aligned with her needs and her vision for the
business. To do that, I provided Frank with a checklist that
showed where each different type of expense needed to appear
in the reports. He was also charged with *maintaining* that list
going forward, which meant that if he received anything from
the team that didn't fit into the pre-defined checklist, he would
ask questions of the team members, including Nathalie, until
he knew how to categorize the transaction in a way that would
be meaningful to Nathalie.

The keys to having meaningful information at your
fingertips are to:

- Understand your net income by line of business
- Pay attention to changes in your Cash Flow Statement
- Format the key reporting line items so that they show the relevant trends

* * *

Nathalie's bookkeeping frustrations are shared by many of today's small business owners. I hope you've seen by now that these frustrations are preventable! Sometimes, all it takes is a few tweaks to the current system.

Our next step will be to begin using this valuable information to create a forecast, so you can take a look into the future.

CHAPTER 3

Look Ahead: Forecasting

Business owners lose valuable sleep over what may happen in the future, and Nathalie was no exception. There are external threats, internal weaknesses, unrealized visions, the unpredictability of team members, and so many other factors and variables waiting to reveal themselves on the far side of *right now*.

You can't control the future, but – with the right information – you can influence your company's *place* in the future.

A few days after her first review of the newly formatted financial statements, Nathalie reached out to me. She sounded much less frustrated than she had during our previous calls and meetings. When I asked how things were going, she said, "Great. Now I can fully relate to everything the financial statements are reporting." More importantly, her gut feelings about the business had been substantiated by the numbers in the reports, so it was much easier to talk about her business with investors, customers, vendors, and employees. Also, since Nathalie had made the changes to accelerate cash flow into the business, she no longer needed to consider a loan.

But all of that progress begged the next question: What could all of that data tell Nathalie about what was coming down the road? Everything we had discussed to that point had been about looking backward. Those three main reports consisted of a snapshot (the Balance Sheet) and videos (P&L and Cash Flow Statement) of what had happened *last* month (or last year). Although it was a huge relief to have that perspective in the bag, she wanted to talk about looking ahead.

The real value of knowing and understanding your company's financial history is in how it informs your company's future.

In Nathalie's case, she knew that the best and highest use of her time was in steering the ship to mitigate risks and seize opportunities. She knew she needed more information to be able to do that. So I got another lunch invitation (yes, food is that important).

Key Performance Indicators

During our lunch meeting, Nathalie and I talked about the future. She wanted to be facing forward with enhanced visibility. We talked about something she'd been using regularly in RunTrue's operations, but not with the financials: key performance indicators, or KPIs (which we'll talk about more fully in Chapter 5).

> **You can't predict the future, but key performance indicators (KPIs) provide a guidance system.**

KPIs act very much like the buoys and channel markers that ship captains use to get feedback. Captains can't always *see* what's ahead when it's hazy or stormy on the water, but they *do* have reference points they can use to calculate exactly where they are in any moment. In addition, they can rest assured that if they aim at the next milestone (KPI result) that they *can* see, then they're at least headed in the right overall direction, and will remain within intended boundaries (i.e., toward their ultimate destination). Based on instrument readings and landmarks, they can make *very educated guesses* about what's coming and how they should adapt to it. In short, they can forecast.

Nathalie needed a guidance system so that she could forecast more accurately.

The good news is that the two financial reports we discussed in the previous chapter (Chapter 2) hold the key to obtaining this forecast. This holds true for any company, even those with the most basic bookkeeping systems.

Forecasting Basics

There are two types of forecasts. One is the *budget* that is traditionally created once a year and focuses on the P&L for the coming year. It uses recent trends and future assumptions to make a solid case for what to expect of the financial statements in the coming months. That's all well and good, but it needed a couple of added tweaks to become truly valuable to Nathalie.

The second type of forecast, most useful for companies that are more tightly cash-strapped (but never a bad idea to have in place), is a 13-week *detailed* cash flow forecast (which I will introduce in the next main section).

My suggestion to use a forecasting model came as no surprise to Nathalie. She had been keeping something like that on the back of a napkin for the previous three months. But then, every time she saw the actual bank balance, she realized there were a few things she had missed in her attempts at forecasting. And she got tired of pulling the napkins out of the dryer every time they went through the laundry, requiring her to start all over.

Creating a traditional monthly or yearly budget is a popular exercise, but, unfortunately, many business owners stop there. Nathalie had already been through the process of creating RunTrue's annual budget, so the hardest part was done.

Those budgets become useful tools only when they are integrated into monthly business reporting systems, and updated in a way that retains their history while keeping them relevant. Let's go a little deeper to see how that happens.

Using Assumptions and Variations

We started with three sets of data: 1) the financial reports (Balance Sheet, Income Statement, Cash Flow Reports), 2) trend reporting, and 3) Nathalie's vision for the business – what she'd always wanted to try, what her gut has told her would work. With those in hand, we took some time to create a flexible forecasting model that could be easily adapted to the various budget scenarios that Nathalie wanted to evaluate.

What made that forecasting so useful were the assumptions involved. During our lunch conversation, Nathalie came up with her assumptions, and with as many variations of those assumptions as she wanted to explore.

The financial reports and Nathalie's assumptions provided everything needed over the next week to create the relevant key performance indicators (KPIs).

The outcomes of various future scenarios we looked at – each presented in a clear and fully integrated format –provided the most important thing Nathalie needed: clarity about what each of those variations would do to cash flow and the bank balance. And that allowed her to make informed decisions.

An integrated budget or forecast provides insights into how business decisions will most likely affect future cash flow and bank balances.

Yes, budgeting is time-consuming. But it can be much more useful if you also come up with and clarify your key assumptions for the coming year. This is crucial. Most businesses put in the time for budgeting once a year, but the resulting document is often only printed out, placed on a shelf, and then forgotten.

Nathalie's business budget was no exception. That budget book, for all of the hard work and time that went into it, had been doing nothing to help her run the business on an ongoing basis. All that work was for naught, because, as the saying goes, "The budget was obsolete as soon as it was printed."

When Nathalie mentioned that her budget was obsolete, I challenged her a bit (carefully, because she *was* buying my lunch): "Nathalie, the budget you already have isn't obsolete. It provides as clear a picture as it's possible to have before you launch into this new year's initiatives."

Things may change constantly, but the outputs from the budgeting process are still useful.

Sure enough, Nathalie admitted that the budget *was* based on some very clear assumptions, *was* properly documented by the accountant and the bookkeeper, and *could be* easily adjusted in future forecasts as additional information came to light. Also, I pointed out, it held the baseline information to which she could compare what went better or worse than she'd expected.

Month by month, by making comparisons to the original budget, Nathalie could determine whether:

- Her assumptions were flawed
- Operations were doing better or worse than she'd expected them to
- Processes were broken
- The business environment had changed
- A combination of the factors was producing an unexpected result

Just like it was for Nathalie, this information about your own business is critical for you to have, because it gives you the ability to adjust your expectations for the future, based on what you know and where you are right now.

When you understand why you're missing or exceeding your original budget, you can make an informed adjustment to your operations or to your expectations.

Forecasting allows you to simulate moving the levers of your business a bit here and there to adjust its course. This works the same way as a weather change that prompts a ship's captain to pull a little to starboard in order to keep his heading and still arrive at the planned destination.

As a business owner myself, I can't imagine a more comforting thought. Nathalie confirmed this as she was paying the lunch bill. She said, "My forecasts will never be wholly accurate, but the difference now is that my predictions will be well informed, *and* I'll know quickly if there's anything internal that I need to fix in order to stay on track."

Setting up the Model

After lunch, I used an Excel template to set up a forecasting model that tied Nathalie's budgeted financial statements together in a way that guaranteed that any change in assumptions would be properly reflected in *all three* financial statements. This is a powerful tool that you can have a bookkeeper or accountant set up. Creating it involved inputting the current P&L and Balance Sheet budgets into the template, with a few formulas that would calculate changes in budgeted cash flow.

That model became the tool for Nathalie to use to evaluate any scenario she wanted to throw at it.

With all of that information in one model that linked the financial reports together, Nathalie could see for each of the coming twelve months and for each of the business assumptions she made (or tested):

- When and how much cash would flow out of the business
- When and how much cash would flow into the business
- The balance in the business checking account
- The predicted profitability of her business

Setting up the model for the first time will likely require someone in the accounting and finance field to input some data and basic formulas for you. However, once the model is established, you can do as Nathalie did. Her existing finance lead person simply updated it each month, interpreted her assumptions for each scenario she wanted to explore, and delivered an updated long-term cash flow forecast as the year progressed.

As business realities change, the forecast model can easily be updated to keep a clear eye on the future.

Only Four Questions

I got Nathalie started with her forecasting model, setting it up to generate the reporting she needed to keep the forecasting relevant all year. To do the set-up I needed her original monthly budget for the year, plus four additional assumptions, plus some historical averages that I provided. The set-up only took five minutes of Nathalie's time.

Below are the four assumptions I asked Nathalie to decide on. She could change her assumptions in the model to explore different forecasted outcomes.

1. What is the *average* length of time you wanted to take to pay you suppliers' bills?
2. What is the *average* length of time it will realistically take your customers to pay you after they've been invoiced? (This will not necessarily be the same as the payment terms shown on the invoices.)
3. How long do you intend to hold your inventory (*on average*) before you convert it into product and sell it to your customers?
4. How much per month do you plan to spend on purchasing new fixed assets?

With that information in hand, I had everything required to create a model that reflected Nathalie's assumptions and any business changes she wanted to make in the following 12 months. I sat with her in her office and showed her how to use it. It didn't take long.

"That's it?" Nathalie asked.

"Yes. You'll only need to update your assumptions about those four issues each month, as well as discuss with your team any changes in direction you want to take, or any operational realities that have emerged.

That gave her a robust forecasting process that tied back to cash flow *and* her gut instincts about the business. She had everything she needed to value RunTrue, plan for the future, tweak her operations, and grow her business profitably without running out of cash.

With a good forecasting system, you can clearly see when cash shortages or excesses are predicted, and make solid decisions about investing and borrowing.

Suddenly, Nathalie could predict, by month, and for the first time:

- How much each month to draw from or pay back to the credit line
- Whether a different source of borrowed funds made more sense

- How much money she herself would put into and draw out of the business

Your budget can be more than a paperweight. Properly utilized, it sets milestones for achieving your vision.

I want to make it clear that the original budget itself doesn't change as the year progresses. But it *is* relevant. The key is to save it and put it into whatever system is necessary to show you each month how your *actual* operations are performing, as compared to the original budget for each month.

With those variances clearly laid out, you are ready to put the forecasting model to work.

What's Working and What's Not

Using the model, you can clearly see where things are working and where they're not working, and whether they're working as you expected. You can drill down to the specific issues, behaviors, processes, and systems that are either exceeding, meeting, or not meeting your expectations.

After you review your forecast each month, update it for the coming months based on new realities. Doing this every month will take only a one-hour time commitment from you.

Your accounting lead can enter in the changes, and it will automatically update the monthly cash flow forecast.

What to Generate Each Month

The key is to have your accounting lead save the following documents in each month's closing folder (whether it's a physical or digital folder):

- A full year budget by month
- A full year of actuals for each month
- An updated forecast created after each month's close

That will make available to you the full spectrum of financial information, both backward-looking and forward-looking, in a format that links it to your vision of the business.

Here's a sample outline of the information your financial team should prepare for you each month, and when it should be prepared:

1. At the start of the year – January 1

    a.   A 12-column monthly budget for January –
December of the coming year

2.   At the end of January
    a.   Actual performance for January
    b.   Forecasted performance for February – December
    c.   January actual performance compared to the
original budget created at before the beginning of
the year

3.   At the end of February
    a.   Actual performance for January – February
    b.   Forecast performance for March – December
    c.   Compared to the original budget for January –
December

4.   And the same as above for each month thereafter,
until…

5.   At the end of December
    a.   Actual performance for January – December
    b.   Compared to the original budget for January –
December

After I had helped Nathalie to put that process into place, it involved Nathalie for less than an hour each month going forward. She had all of that accumulating information at her fingertips, though, and she could look it over any time she wanted to know how the business was doing compared to the original budget, and how she felt it would do for the rest of the year. These two key pieces of information gave Nathalie the confidence to support her (usually correct) gut instincts about the business. But they also let her know – in a very timely, transparent, relevant, and reliable fashion – if she got off track from her plan.

13-Week Cash Flow Forecast

Let's take a step away from the financial statements and the model above now and look at the second type of financial forecast, the 13-week cash flow forecast. In Nathalie's case, this second forecast was critical, because she had very tight cash flows (cash bounced around close to a zero balance, with very large cash swings in each month). The 13-week cash flow forecast is different from a monthly forecast, because it predicts every deposit to be made and every check that's going to be written in the coming weeks.

Getting this forecast model set up is simply a matter of asking the bookkeeper to set up a spreadsheet that looks like the one shown below (also available as a spreadsheet at http://bit.ly/ yourfirstcfo_cashflow).

	B	C	D	E	F	G
1						
2	**SMALL BUSINESS CASH FLOW PROJECTION**					
3	Demo Company					
4						
5	Starting date	3/26/2016				
6	Cash balance alert minimum	$100,000.00				
7			ACTUAL	ACTUAL	ACTUAL	FORECAST	FOREC
8		Beginning	3/26/2016	4/2/2016	4/9/2016	4/16/2016	
9	Cash on hand (beginning of week)	$222,112.69	$222,112.69	$178,281.15	$258,383.63	$283,340.49	$2
10	Cash on hand (end of week)	$222,112.69	$178,281.15	$258,383.63	$283,340.49	$270,611.75	$2
11							
12	**CASH RECEIPTS**	Beginning	1	2	3		
13	Cash sales						
14	Returns and allowances						
15	Collections on accounts receivable		$900.00	$239,718.00	$76,000.00		
16	Interest, other income						
17	Loan proceeds						
18	Owner contributions						
19	**TOTAL CASH RECEIPTS**		$900.00	$239,718.00	$76,000.00	$0.00	
20	Total cash available	$222,112.69	$223,012.69	$417,999.15	$334,383.63	$283,340.49	$
21							
22	**CASH PAID OUT**	Beginning					
23	Credit Card Payment			$10,001.00		$10,000.00	
24	Contract labor Jennifer					$1,500.00	
25	Contract labor Tom						
26	Employee benefit programs			$13,014.80			
27	Insurance (other than health)			$1,015.01			
28	Office expense						
29	Rent or lease						
30	Supplies (not in COGS)						
31	Taxes and licenses						
32	Wages (less emp. credits)		$44,731.54	$13,871.96	$33,734.54	$1,228.74	
33	Lineberry						
34	Met Life						
35	Hartford						
36	Sentinel						
37	Biofortis						
38	Kate Kessler						
39	Truefit						
40	Wynick Robbins						
41	Miscellaneous / Bill.com (Actual)			$121,712.75	$17,308.60		
42	**SUBTOTAL**		$44,731.54	$159,615.52	$51,043.14	$12,728.74	
43	Loan principal payment						
44	Capital purchases						
45	**TOTAL CASH PAID OUT**		$44,731.54	$159,615.52	$51,043.14	$12,728.74	
46	Cash on hand (end of month)	$222,112.69	$178,281.15	$258,383.63	$283,340.49	$270,611.75	$

This forecast is maintained by the bookkeeper from week to week (or from day to day, in critical cases) via a reconciliation of the bank statement. In this reconciliation, the bookkeeper replaces each week's forecasted amounts with the *actual* amounts of cash received, cash paid out, and the new cash balance. The bookkeeper then adds a new 13th week, and updates the forecast for the upcoming weeks, to reflect the resulting changes in assumed receipts and disbursements.

Most bookkeepers are not hired to keep this sort of information up to date, so you may need to convert one of your in-house people to learn and maintain the 13-week forecasting model – or expand your contract with your bookkeeper to include it. Although this model maintenance does not require an accounting or bookkeeping set of skills, it does require that the person doing it is: 1) comfortable using Excel (or another spreadsheet product), 2) someone you trust with access to seeing your banking information, and 3) reviewed by someone else (internally or externally) who can validate the spreadsheet's integrity.

As a fallback, Nathalie's QuickBooks *could* have been configured and maintained in a way that made doing a weekly cash-flow forecast automatic. That *is* something that she could have required of her bookkeeper, but to set it up properly, it would likely have required participation by a higher-level financial lead. Nathalie and I talked it over and I shared with her that the QuickBooks report would not be as easy to read or adjust as an Excel-type model that could handle some of the exceptions that inevitably come up.

Nathalie implemented my recommendation, which was to have someone pull the relevant data from QuickBooks and the bank, and then generate a user-friendly, Excel-based 13-week cash flow forecast. That allowed it to be set up in a way that made the most sense to her. Every business owner likes to see things a little bit differently, and every business has exceptions that QuickBooks or any other off-the-shelf accounting system isn't set up to handle. So, Excel usually makes the most sense. Once that spreadsheet was complete, Nathalie started reviewing it weekly, and she was thrilled to have such a clear look at her immediate cash runway.

The 13-week cash flow forecast report is *only and all about cash*. The actual bank balance at the beginning of the current week is recorded, then all the expected, upcoming receipts and payments are recorded in the thirteen weekly columns. As the weeks pass, the actual receipts and payments are input in place of the forecasted numbers, and the coming weeks are adjusted accordingly.

With the implementation of the new 13-week cash flow forecast, Nathalie could go to bed each night with confidence that she'd know the expected ending balance of the bank account within a *very* small margin of error, week after week.

This report would normally be laid out in a landscape orientation showing all 13 weeks as the columns. The key is that you can see, for the end of each week, the projected cash balance in the bank account. That way, if you see a point at which it dips lower than you like, you can adjust some of your business levers by:

- Deferring payments
- Accelerating collections
- Borrowing funds
- Investing funds
- Changing the timing of upcoming controllable discretionary business expenses

Nathalie quickly saw that the information provided by the weekly cash flow forecast was invaluable. In combination with the upgraded monthly closing process, and in much less time than she'd formerly invested on financials, she was sitting with a clear view into her company's future.

She also had a more reliable prediction of cash funding needs and payback options from and to her credit lines.

* * *

I have utilized and refined the traditional budget forecasting process and the 13-week cash flow forecast during my career. Although the format has changed, and the systems for generating the data vary, this forecasting system works consistently for businesses of all sizes and levels of maturity. Through the process of refining the tools, I've learned something important about forecasting models.

The success of forecasting models and concepts is not limited by company size or complexity.

Although forecasting models can vary in their cost and fancy delivery methods, for the cost of having two spreadsheets set up you can minimize your tactical involvement in *gathering the data* and maximize the strategic value you receive from your accounting and reporting process – value extracted from finally having a reliable way to evaluate and improve your business' cash flow.

CHAPTER 4

Meet Your Cash: Controls Over Cash

One of the most used words in all my conversations with Nathalie was *cash*. It's the most used word in my conversations with all of my clients. This is because cash demands the attention of every business owner.

Cash is king, which means it deserves the surest of possible controls.

Nathalie knew that her bank account couldn't ever have less than a zero balance. If that happened she would have to close her doors and file for some sort of bankruptcy protection. Then she would have had to dig in for an onslaught of jurisdictional and legal inquiries.

Nathalie – like every other business owner – knew the basic goal of business, at its most complex and fascinating, as well as at its simple best.

> **The goal of doing business is to get the highest return possible, at the lowest possible risk, for every unit of cash invested.**

Cash is king at both ends of the business cycle: up front, when cash is initially invested, and later, when cash is earned and turned back in to the business or returned to investors.

This chapter is an important supplement to the progress we made in setting up Nathalie's books and organization for financial clarity. Everything we have discussed so far relates to how Nathalie's financial statements were configured to tell her *the story of her cash*. She was getting used to using the new systems and it was making a difference.

It was time to take breather from setting up systems and processes and show Nathalie what she could do periodically to gain an even deeper understanding of her company's cash story.

I proposed that she commit to the following practices, shared with me by one of my former CEOs.

- Sign every check for one month in every year.
- Balance the checkbook once a year.

Let's explore each of these practices in a bit more detail.

For One Month, Sign Every Check

I suggested to Nathalie that, once a year, for a whole month, she herself sign every check that left the company. Certainly, in a lot of companies, checks aren't physically signed anymore, so in some cases *sign every check* is a metaphor for *review and approve every payment that leaves your company's bank account*. It doesn't matter how big or small the amount of the check is. I suggested that Nathalie review every single one.

Nathalie learned more about her growing organization from that single exercise than from any employee-shadowing exercise she'd done, from any regular meeting she'd attended, or from any process review she'd studied.

I shared with Nathalie a story about the CEO who had taught me this practice. As the incoming CEO, in only *one month* of signing the checks at her new company – she uncovered all of the issues noted below (and more that are not listed). I joined that company as CFO just after she completed the process, and her results replaced a significant swath of my typical initial control review, identifying:

- Duplicate subscriptions for industry magazines
- Processes that required multiple levels of redundant approvals
- Invoices sitting on desks unattended to
- Expenditures that people thought they could authorize but that they truly weren't supposed to
- Lack of negotiation on large contracts
- Key industry information that wasn't getting disseminated to the people in the organization who most needed it
- A room full of paper files, all of which had already been scanned
- Documents scanned by both an internal process and then also sent for third-party scanning
- Exorbitant copy machine leasing fees
- Money being spent because "the CEO said to," when, in fact, the CEO never had said to
- Because of the checks she *didn't* see that month, she learned that a couple of employees were paying money out of their own pockets to provide treats for

employees but they had never been reimbursed, or even recognized, for it

That is only a partial list of her discoveries – but you get the point. This exercise gives you visibility into every corner of your organization, because it puts you in direct contact with the oil that keeps the engine running: *cash*.

Nathalie very quickly understood the magnitude of information that she could gain by doing this exercise – information that no other report or analysis would provide.

This exercise was so helpful because it put Nathalie nose-to-nose with RunTrue's cash flow, which was how it had been when she'd started her business. As the organization grew, the things that Nathalie couldn't see directly also expanded. For the one month that she took the time for this practice, it removed all the layers between her and RunTrue's cash.

Balance the Checkbook

Another great way to get up close with cash is to randomly pick one month a year to balance the checkbook yourself or to review the bank reconciliation in detail. I suggested that Nathalie pick her month, which she did. That month, she had Frank (or she could have done it with her accountant) walk her through that month's bank statement reconciliation. I advised Nathalie to seek to fully understand the reasoning behind:

- Every check that had been written but hadn't cleared the bank
- Any check that had cleared the bank, but – for whatever reason – wasn't reflected in the financial statements
- Any deposits that had hit the bank but weren't showing in the financial statements
- Any deposits that were showing in the financial statements but hadn't hit the bank
- Any bank entry for which the description wasn't clear

If Nathalie wasn't 100% satisfied with her understanding of every single one of those categories – if she didn't understand them perfectly, in language that made sense to her – I advised her to stop the process and get a second opinion from a finance lead or accountant who was not in the normal chain of command.

Never accept an answer of, "It's just a timing thing," from your bookkeeper or accountant when you are discussing cash.

As Nathalie and I discussed this issue, I realized that it may have seemed like an overreaction to stop the review process and seek answers elsewhere. And it may seem that way to you, as well. When I explained more, Nathalie realized the reasoning behind it was something that she already knew:

- The bank account is the lifeblood of the company
- The bank account is the point at which she (and every business owner) is most vulnerable.
- Although many things in accounting can and should be rounded up so they can be talked about at a much higher level, *cash* recording is not one of them!

Cash is simple. When cash comes into the bank account, that should be reflected in your bookkeeping accounts. When cash leaves the bank, that should be reflected in your bookkeeping accounts. Period.

* * *

What was important for Nathalie about those two exercises were the things they highlighted for her:

- Every check written should have been one she'd expected to be written.
- There was never a legitimate excuse for a bank account to have an unreconciled difference.

In accounting, many things aren't black and white. However, when taking a raw, unfiltered look at cash through the two practices in this chapter, things *are* black and white; and the CEO should ask questions until she feels 100% comfortable and there are no grey areas.

Nathalie understood that if the answers she got from doing these practices didn't *feel* black and white, then it might be time for her to get some outside financial advice.

Don't accept any uneasy feelings when it comes to cash. If something doesn't make sense to *you*, dig deeper.

CHAPTER 5

Gain Insight: More about Key Performance Indicators

We briefly touched on key performance indicators (KPIs) in Chapter 3. The culmination and highest purpose of your work to get accounting and reporting streamlined is that you come to a place where you can readily measure, analyze, and predict information that is crucial to you and your company. Let's call those three rewards PAM, for short:

- Predict
- Analyze

- Measure

They're listed above in order of their value to you and your company, and in reverse order of their execution.

The ultimate reward for investing in a solid accounting and reporting process is an accurate, reliable, simple, and timely dashboard of *only* and *all* the information that is critical to *you*.

Nathalie had put several improvements in place – and their implementation hadn't required anywhere near the aggravation she'd anticipated. By providing a little direction to her finance team, Nathalie had:

- Cleaned up her financial statements so that they aligned with her business
- Set herself up to see trends within her business
- Forecasted revenue, net income, and cash flow monthly, with a full-year view and a shorter-term view of each 13 weeks

- Identified and removed a lot of wasteful spending, through a one-month detailed review of check-writing
- Set up an annual meeting with her bookkeeper to walk through balancing her bank account for a month

In addition, and more importantly, Nathalie had also provided her banker with the information he needed to validate her gut instinct that the business was well-positioned to obtain financing should she choose to expand RunTrue's product portfolio.

Nathalie had come a long, long way on the journey of owning her financials with confidence. On that morning when she and I first talked, as she was pacing in her office, that level of confidence and lack of frustration was inconceivable to her. Back then, she'd been unsure of any of the key drivers of her current financial situation, and yet spent more than 16 hours a month buried in financial reports.

With the new practices and systems in place, Nathalie slept at night and only devoted two hours a month to reviewing financial reports and providing input for updating the forecast. Yet she had key information to rely on any time she needed it.

What Nathalie did was to convert her finance and accounting team from a business *expense* into a business *asset*. No longer did Frank only keep the records using an old template that didn't align with the business – and then forward the file to the accountant to use for doing the taxes. Instead, Nathalie was intercepting the reports and extracting critical value from them. The system performed the three PAM functions – predicting, analyzing, and measuring – with reliable efficiency, accuracy, and in a timely manner. In short, Nathalie had a dashboard from which to run her business.

Don't be scared off if you don't have a team in your business. Sometimes *the team* is made up of one very talented bookkeeper (and there are a lot of them out there). Sometimes the team is a full-fledged internal accounting department. Most times, the team is something in between those two extremes.

For *prediction*, *analysis,* and *measurement* to add value to Nathalie's business, the basic variables in the reporting stream needed to be inescapably tied to providing her feedback that was completely aligned with her corporate strategy and objectives.

- She needed to be able to *predict* what certain strategic initiatives would do to her numbers (most importantly, to her cash flow).
- In order to *predict*, she needed her team to *analyze* how those initiatives were performing against Nathalie's original estimates.

- In order to *analyze*, her team needed to *measure* the results of those initiatives.

Before we had set up the processes to serve that purpose, it would have been impossible for Nathalie's bookkeeping and accounting team to add net value to the organization. The tendency for her outsourced bookkeeping service to constrain her to a fixed template for reporting kept Nathalie from getting information that was aligned with her business model. For Nathalie, and for every business owner or CEO, this alignment is *the* thing that makes financial information useful.

Even with all we'd done, Nathalie was still a little frustrated that there wasn't a quicker way to assess the performance of the business – at least the key business levers – in a more efficient fashion. As it was, she could look at the financial statements in the 12-month spreadsheet to evaluate trends and variances. But she wished she could evaluate the impact of her decisions by using only one or two numbers, because that would give her a quick hit of whether she was off-base or not as she directed the company.

Highlighting the connection between your business operations and key items on your financial statements is an important step toward gaining confidence that the actions you take can be measured and reported back to you accurately, and in a way that you can adjust as necessary.

This is where we resume our discussion of key performance indicators, first mentioned in Chapter 3. KPIs speak directly to *why* you are in business – for that reason, they are powerful tools.

> **It is important to define the key performance indicators (KPIs) that best represent your goals and vision for your business.**

KPIs give you easy access to the most pertinent information about your business, in a context that aligns with your strategy and allows you to react more quickly to business realities.

Whether you've done so formally or informally, you've made strategic plans, identifying the milestones you want to achieve as you work to maximize the value of your investment (or your investors' investment) in your business. The financial statements we've already discussed provide the information required to evaluate your performance against many of those milestones. KPIs add another layer of control.

There are hundreds of different metrics that can be used as KPIs, but four important ratios provide answers to the most basic questions about your business. These metrics are so crucial that every business owner should understand them, at least in concept. We'll talk more about them in a moment.

Other possible KPIs can also be explored, and you can get ideas about which ones would be most appropriate for you and your business by learning what KPIs your competitors use, and involving your finance team to calculate them and include them in their reports to you.

The four ratios I discuss here are *contribution margin percentage*, *days sales outstanding*, *days payables outstanding*, and the *inventory conversion ratio*. I'll introduce and explain each one in its own section below.

To be relevant, a KPI (whether one of the four I mentioned above or any others) needs to be compared to:

- Your internal expectations for that metric
- The industry benchmarks for that metric
- The trend you are seeing in that metric

Performance in those three contexts are what make your actual metrics meaningful. A KPI number by itself doesn't mean anything. No KPI has value in isolation.

The overlap of the three spheres of internal expectations, industry benchmarks, and trends will vary, and the importance of each one relative to your specific business may vary. But understanding the behavior of the basic four KPIs in the context of these spheres is the key to aligning measurements with your strategy.

In a perfect world, every component of your business strategy would have at least one KPI by which to measure its success or failure; and every one of those KPIs would be predicted, analyzed, and measured against trends, expectations, and the competition.

Every month, when your financials are delivered accurately, and in a timely fashion, with the key numbers highlighted, it takes only one small further step for your team to habitually calculate and provide the actual performance of each of the KPIs at the close of the month. With this information in hand, you can adjust the ship's heading as you go, month by month without having to look at every financial statement trend yourself.

Each of the four core KPIs is presented below, with an explanation of its purpose, and then a demonstration of how that KPI provides insight to CEOs and process-owners. For CEOs, the core KPIs allow them to direct their finance teams to deliver more pertinent information. A process-owner is the person who oversees a business, department, or a section of the business. In a one-person business, the process-owner is the CEO herself. For the process-owners, the core KPIs allow them to adjust the business lever (or activity) that is causing a disruption to a trend, or causing a less than favorable outcome as compared to expectations or industry averages.

This next part of the book is the most intense, but there are only four KPIs, and once you know how to use them, you'll be glad you kept reading. So power through the next short sections (and come back to them later as a reference manual). Nathalie survived learning about the core KPIs, and it only required one glass of wine to recover after a half-hour of study.

It is important to remember that all four of these KPIs are generated from numbers that are *already* in your existing financial reports. This is shown in the middle column of the graphic in each section below.

Contribution Margin Percentage

The higher the contribution margin, the better. It is calculated for each product or service line, to show what percentage of revenue is left after deducting the costs of generating that revenue.

The contribution margin tells you what percentage of your sales price is left over to *contribute* to covering fixed expenses after paying the product or service costs.

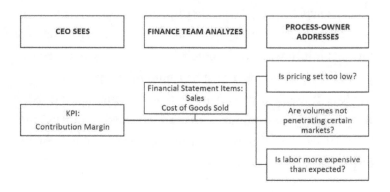

Gross Profit / Revenue = Contribution Margin

CEO SEES

FINANCE TEAM ANALYZES

PROCESS-OWNER ADDRESSES

KPI:
Contribution Margin

Financial Statement Items:
Sales
Cost of Goods Sold

Is pricing set too low?

Are volumes not penetrating certain markets?

Is labor more expensive than expected?

Days Sales Outstanding (DSO)

The lower the DSO the better. Your DSO is the number of days it takes your customers to pay you for invoiced sales (keeping in mind that you are purposely allowing them some number of these days in your terms of payment).

Your days sales outstanding (DSO) tells you how long someone else is using *your* money.

(Accounts Receivable/Sales) * 365 = DSO

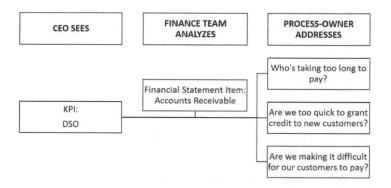

Days Payables Outstanding (DPO)

The higher the DPO, the better. Your DPO represents how quickly you send cash out to your vendors.

Days payable outstanding (DPO) tells you how long you are using someone else's money.

Gross Profit / Revenue = Contribution Margin

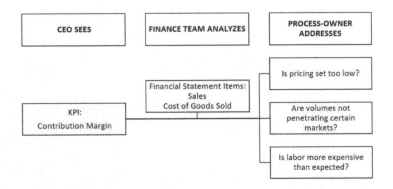

Inventory Conversion Ratio

The lower the inventory conversion ratio, the better. This KPI represents how quickly you use up the inventory for which you have already put out cash.

The inventory conversion ratio calculates how long after a purchase of inventory materials and labor it takes to *convert* products to sales.

(Accounts Payable/Expenses) * 365 = Number of days in which you pay your vendors

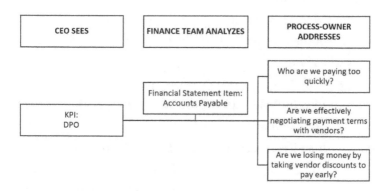

Other KPIs

There are many other KPI options, and their importance varies according to the business model used, company size, financing structure, and industry sector.

When using additional metrics, the process of identifying what numbers the CEO or business owner wants to see is the same as indicated in the graphics in the four sections above. First, figure out what the CEO wants to keep tabs on; second, figure out what the financial team needs to analyze; and, third, work back from that to the questions the process-owner needs to be able to answer.

We already completed a good bit of the groundwork for this deep dive during the Chapter 1 exercise of Drawing Your Business where you outlined your vision for the company.

As a business owner and/or CEO, you will create meaningful KPIs when you:

- Identify what key processes are operating in the organization
- Identify the activities that drive those processes
- Forecast how much you want those processes to deliver and, subsequently, how the specific activities must perform to achieve those results

To finish up the process of creating a meaningful KPI, the finance team needs to:

- Identify the financial statement items that reflect those activities and then forecast them based on how they must perform
- Determine what ratios or combinations of those financial statement items will give you meaningful KPIs
- Create the forecast for desired KPI values, then compare monthly KPI actual performance to that value every month

* * *

Before we leave the issue of KPIs and move on to building your finance team, let's take a step back and look at things from a different perspective for a moment. An important takeaway from this chapter is that the value of your KPI reporting depends on your bookkeeping.

> ***How*** **your bookkeeper captures information about your business is the key that drives all successful reporting.**

The groundwork you did in Drawing Your Business is so important, because it sets up the framework for helping your bookkeeper capture information effectively.

If your financial reports are merely flying past your desk on the way from your bookkeeper to your accountant, or if you are drowning in reports that you ignore, then you are losing everything valuable about the bookkeeping work for which you are paying.

If the process described in this book is set up properly; if the inputs are correct at the source; and if the bookkeeper has defined your books in a way that is meaningful to your view of your business, based on your business model, then useful KPIs can be delivered to you in a timely fashion each month. Any company performance issues will be easily identified by you, and solutions or investigations very quickly assigned for analysis and repair.

Nathalie quickly learned that with the KPI figures in hand, she had the highest level of feedback for steering the company. She could see everything she needed to see. For the items that looked out of sync, it was in the hands of the finance and operations groups to identify the source of the problem when processes didn't perform as expected.

Since your KPIs will align with your company strategy, clearly communicate to your team how your KPIs connect to very specific business processes. This gives the team the opportunity to see how adjusting the processes leads to changes in the KPI the following month.

You, as the CEO, are responsible for validating that the levers of the business are coordinated in any proposed improvement, and for making any further adjustments needed to keep the company on course toward achieving its vision. That is the goal – whether your business is a one-person shop or a $500-million organization.

As the business owner, your time is best spent doing the things only you can do. Your team can do the work of generating

KPIs, so that they are captured, measured, monitored, adjusted, and remeasured habitually. Let them do that, and put the captain of the ship where she belongs: at the helm, setting the course and using the high-level accounting tools – the KPIs – to assess risks and make adjustments as necessary.

CHAPTER 6

Build Your Team: Finance and Accounting Roles

A question most small- to medium-size businesses face at one time or another, usually when they are ready to grow and move to the next level, is "Do I need a CFO?"

The answer can be complicated, because good CFOs are expensive, and there isn't a blueprint for how to find the right person for your business. Therefore, it's useful to have some guidance around figuring out whether you really need one.

You may need a CFO if you feel alone at the top, and need someone you trust to talk over the big questions.

Nathalie gained incredible clarity and confidence by optimizing her financial and accounting processes. But my phone did ring again with a call from her, six months later. She was extremely tired, and told me that her board meeting was coming up. Her question for me was simple: "Do I need a CFO?"

The "big questions" that CFOs can help with usually aren't only about the finances or even only about the business. For many business owners, the questions CFOs help them answer can also cover their financial interests in the business and their personal and family financial situations.

When Nathalie called me, she was in the midst of considering a variety of options and issues: company growth, an exit plan, the salary she was drawing, attracting the right employees, and where to invest the cash that had been piling up as a result of her business' amazing success over the previous six months. She knew that a fast-growing, medium-sized company was a blessing, but it was also a challenge. Nathalie had good ideas about financing, an investor, a target to acquire, and a potential buyer, but she needed someone she could trust to discuss and debate the complexities of those critical decisions.

You may need a CFO when you need informed answers and can't afford to play roulette with crucial decisions.

The decision to bring on a CFO – either part-time or full-time, or even just on an interim basis – often isn't an obvious or easy one. From my perspective, and backed by my 25 years of experience in the fields of accounting and finance, the easiest way to address the CFO issue is to ask yourself this question: *Would a CFO bring a return on the investment in their salary?*

If a CFO would bring more savings or increase income enough to produce a return on the investment in their salary, it could be time to hire one.

This is a great concept – but it is much easier to ask the question than to answer it.

When I worked with Nathalie, instead of jumping directly into trying to answer the question, I first walked her through a few preliminary questions, to help her put the main question about hiring a CFO into context, and to focus her decision-making.

These are the questions I asked her:

- Are you spending more than 10 to 15% of your time on the company (and your own) finances?
- Do you have sufficient policies in place around who can sign checks, approve purchase orders, commit to contracts, spend money, and deal with cash?
- Is the company big enough that you are removed from the day-to-day activities?
- Are you uncertain about whether everything (and everyone) in your system is protecting your interests?
- Are you uncertain about how you're pricing your products and services?
- Have you received communications from any governmental jurisdictions?
- Has the nature of your business transactions, or the market in which you compete, grown more complex?
- Do your plans for the business cost more than the operating cash you have on hand?
- Are you building up excess cash balances in your business?
- Do you feel alone at the top?

That last question is perhaps the most important one

In Nathalie's case, her answers showed us that it was time for a CFO. There were strategic financial questions she was wrestling with day in and day out, and she had no expert confidant with whom to pressure-test them. In addition, she knew that the company was growing big enough to require more cash; she knew she couldn't see what was going on day-to-day anymore; and she knew she was spending way too much time wrestling with financial decisions.

The issue of being lonely at the top is a situation every CEO or business owner in the world – myself included – can empathize with. Just like Nathalie did, you have an incredible amount of pressure on your shoulders. Your employees, your vendors, your customers, and your family are counting on the decisions you make each day.

A huge portion of that pressure is financial in nature, because you are working to ensure that your business is, and remains, financially viable – or, even better, becomes more financially vibrant. Such topics are often not appropriate to share with most of your stakeholders. Sharing with employees would make them worry. Sharing with customers or vendors would make them assume there were risks they might not want to take.

If you are at that point, wrestling alone with big financial questions, you need a trustworthy person in whom you can confide your concerns, as well as your dreams, for the business.

You need, like Nathalie needed, a trusted sounding board; someone who can help you figure out a way to navigate – without frightening the rest of the organization, your clients, your vendors, or that treasured family of yours. You need someone who has the experience and understanding of your situation to help you filter and sort your concerns; someone who can act as a shock absorber, to insulate the organization from the potential implications of decisions being considered, but who can still work with the team to assist you in navigating the ship forward toward your vision.

"What a comfort that would be. *Yes*. I need that," was Nathalie's conclusion. "But how do we go about finding the right person for me and my business?"

There is one critical component to this decision: Nathalie's CFO choice – whether that CFO was interim, part-time, or full time – absolutely *must* fit in with her company culture in a way that:

- Engenders trust with the team
- Reflects her values
- Drives positive change
- Provides and builds on an air-tight relationship with her

Yes, a CFO's technical skills are critical, as well, but those skills are a given; they're the price a candidate pays to even get to the table. Those skills can be easily verified and tested. However, the relationship Nathalie would have with her CFO, the imprint that person would make on the organization, was the important deciding factor. (Yes, as it happened, I was that right person for Nathalie and her business.)

If your answers to the questions in this chapter didn't point to the need for a CFO, there may still be a need for an additional level of finance expertise in your organization. Below is a brief review of the different levels of support offered by roles in the finance and accounting disciplines.

Before presenting the list in the sections below, I'll clarify that when I use the term *financial lead*, I am referring to the highest level of financial experience that is present in your company or that is providing service to your company.

There are two main variables that determine the level of financial lead required by your company:

- The complexity of your organization and its transactions
- The size of your organization (its revenue, employees, customers, physical footprint)

We can use the analogy of a thermometer. If your business operates with a simple process and is a very small company, you can keep your receipts in a shoe box (though I wouldn't recommend it) and still run a successful business.

Take a look at the graphic (also available at http://prioritiesllc. com/wp-content/uploads/2017/01/Chap6_Thermometer.pdf):

As your company grows in size and complexity, your financial needs – including your need for an increasingly knowledgeable financial lead – will evolve and drive the need to move from a shoe box accounting system to having a bookkeeper. And on up the scale, until your business is large and complex, at which point, you have likely progressed to needing a CFO as the financial lead.

Your business model and the stage your business is in can help you determine the financial lead you and your business need, and can help you find the right fit.

Financial Roles

Here's a breakdown of the most common financial roles and the business stages to which they each are suited.

Bookkeeper

You guessed it: Bookkeepers simply keep the financial books. They record in a tracking system the financial transactions that occur in your accounts, and print off reports that show what they've recorded.

This means they track credits and debits, pay invoices, and apply cash. Bookkeepers are responsible for making sure your financial records are accurate and up-to-date. They may or may not perform bank reconciliations.

Other financial roles will vary from business to business, but – no matter the size or type of your business – you should have a bookkeeper, even if it's you. You can use a bookkeeper who works only as much as is needed to complete the bookkeeping for your business.

Business Accountant

Accountant is a very broad term. It includes certified public accountants (CPAs), who do taxes and audits, but that certification is not required for someone to be called an accountant. And we're not talking about the CFO doing taxes and audits.

Business accountant is the term I use to describe an accountant who is entirely focused on the internal accounting needs of an organization. The role of business accountant can cover some or all the following responsibilities:

- Completing complex account reconciliations
- Generating management-focused financial statements
- Measuring key performance indicators
- Gathering data for more complex reporting
- Managing the bookkeeper

In many cases, business accountants are not CPAs, but they don't necessarily need to be. It's a good idea to ensure that they have, at least, a two-year degree in accounting or a bachelor's degree in accounting to gain comfort that the basics are in place for solid financial reporting.

Financial Analyst

A financial analyst isn't necessarily an accountant type. These folks are usually data jockeys who can take data, both financial and non-financial, from various sources in your business, and integrate it into meaningful reporting for business leaders. Financial analysts have access to the business' raw accounting data, but they don't generally get involved in creating that data; instead, they transform it into meaningful information for business leaders.

A financial analyst will usually have a bachelor's degree in finance or accounting. But don't rule out candidates who are operations leaders, statisticians, math majors, or market researchers.

The translation of data into meaningful information is the key skill for a financial analyst.

Controller

As businesses get larger and more complex, they begin to require the skills of a financial controller. A controller has more experience than an accountant, should have at least bachelor's degree in accounting, and may or may not have a CPA and have experience in a public accounting firm.

The role of a financial controller is evident in the title: They control and protect the assets of a business.

Controllers put the controls in place in your business processes to ensure the protection of your assets and the accurate reporting of your financial performance. The list of what goes into that responsibility is long and involved. If you have a good controller in your organization, you can delegate some of the authority and responsibility for the monthly financial reporting process to them, and rest assured that it is well-tended.

Chief Financial Officer (CFO)

As the heat increases at the top end of the thermometer, you'll graduate to needing a CFO.

The CFO's key roles are to link financial function to business strategy, act as the business' financial liaison, lead by example, and be your fully integrated financial ally, acting on behalf of your entire organization, both internally and externally. The Controller controls and protects your assets, whereas the CFO ensures that they are generating value.

A good CFO will ensure 100% alignment of the finance process with the company's strategy.

Having a CFO in place should allow you to step away from leading the finance and accounting process. With your approval, and with only as much involvement as you *want* to have in that process, they'll hire the staff, align the personnel, manage the budget, and choose the necessary systems for finance and accounting, so that they give you feedback about the business that makes sense to you.

In addition to aligning the financial reporting with how you view the business, they'll also define and report on pivotal performance metrics for the organization. A CFO understands the business levers that are available, and they know how to give you feedback so you to know how much to adjust those levers. In many cases, a CFO will take the lead in working with the relevant teams to make the needed changes.

CFOs understand and can counsel the CEO on the intricacies of finance, treasury, banking, and cash management, as well as risk management. They take responsibility for managing cash flow and protecting the company's assets – finding and ensuring their best and highest use. CFOs are responsible for setting up the business so that the CEO will be able to evaluate and decide on projects and opportunities that will generate the highest possible return on investment (ROI) based on the CEO's risk preferences, and yet be aligned with business strategy.

> **CFOs often fill the role of chief *friend in the foxhole* or chief of staff.**

Your role at the top of your company can be extremely lonely. The most successful CEOs – the ones with the most leveraged business models – usually have trusted CFOs by their sides. These best-of-the-best CEO-CFO teams are built from relationships founded on trust and experience.

CFOs become people with whom CEOs and owners can share visions and concerns, without fearing that the organization will be confused as a result of the discussion.

> **A great CFO is the owner's sounding board, consigliere, and protective perimeter.**

Employing (or outsourcing) someone for a role of this magnitude, may at first feel like giving up too much control, but with the right CFO and with a little time to develop the relationship, having them on board will ultimately free up your time and energy so that you can make the more important decisions and grow your business in a healthy way.

* * *

In a company without sound financial and accounting processes in place:

- There can be a mad scramble at the end of the year for your tax accountant to get what he or she needs for you to stay in compliance with federal, state, and local tax regulations.

- You likely won't see final financial performance data until the end of the year, so you'll be prevented from doing effective tax planning during the year. (With qualified financial support, you could start tax planning discussions six months prior to year-end, and that could make a difference when it comes to tax time.)

- You lose the incredible value of the operational insights that can be gained from data that's aligned with your strategy. This can be a huge lost treasure.

- You miss the opportunity to delegate the oversight of your finances and accounting to someone else so that you can focus on what you do best.

- You can't forecast your cash needs or excesses in a way that lets you take advantage well in advance of things like interest rates or credit lines. You could end up having to get cash in a crisis, which makes it much harder to negotiate good rates. You miss out on opportunities to invest in growth, because it's not clear when you have excess cash.

The plain and simple truth is that engaging appropriate professional financial expertise sets you up for growth and keeps you one step ahead of the game at every stage of your company's life-cycle.

CHAPTER 7

Pick Your CFO: The Range of CFO Choices

Once you've made the decision to retain a CFO, the next step is to fill the role, which requires deciding on what type of CFO you need: full-time, part-time, or interim. There are pros and cons to each of those choices, but there are also characteristics of each option that will help in making the decision.

Nathalie decided that, based on the complexity and size of her business, she needed a CFO. To implement that decision, she first weighed the options regarding what type of CFO, to assess which would be best suited to her and her company's situation.

The different types of CFOs are explained below.

Full-Time CFO

Here's the dilemma: A full-time CFO comes with a full-time salary. As for any role, the compensation and expectations for this role vary according to the experience of the candidate and the geographical scope of the company. CFO gross annual base salaries can be as low as $100,000 for the CFO of a small company, and run up to millions of dollars for CFOs of Fortune 500 companies. In between those extremes is a salary range that applies to most small- to mid-market companies that range in revenue from $10 to $500 million. There are also various options and expectations regarding bonuses, perquisites (freebies), and equity participation.

Below is a helpful outline, using generalized numbers, *addressing only base salary*, that can give you an idea of what might be appropriate for a CFO for your business. Keep in mind that there will also be specific characteristics – of both the company and the CFO candidate – in each situation that influence the numbers below and may cause significant variance from this base.

This outline reflects a consolidation of a variety of salary range guides. For purposes of this discussion, let's assume that the geographical scope of your business is the northeastern United States, and the time frame is 2017.

- Company size: less than $50 million in revenues
  - First-time CFO sample base salary: $120,000/year
  - Experienced CFO sample base salary: $225,000/year
- Company size: between $51 and $100 million
  - First-time CFO sample base salary: $145,000
  - Experienced CFO sample base salary: $300,000
- Company size: between $100 and $250 million
  - First-time CFO sample base salary: $150,000
  - Experienced CFO sample base salary: $375,000
- Company size: between $250 and $500 million
  - First-time CFO sample base salary: $225,000
  - Experienced CFO sample base salary: $495,000

What *is* clear is that hiring a full-time CFO is an expensive choice, so it makes sense to check out what you expect to gain from it, and ensure that the gains will be greater than the costs. Before taking the leap to bring on a full-time CFO, make sure you determine your needs regarding technical skills and experience. Weigh each candidate against those needs, as well as assessing cultural fit with your company and your business style.

Assess the value CFO candidates will add to your business, as well as how they would add it.

Interim and Part-Time CFOs

The costs for interim and part-time CFOs are as varied as the number of candidates you will talk to. Let's explore some generalities and approximate some salary ranges for these types of CFOs.

At the foundation of one proposed calculation is the size of your business revenue. However, there are *many* more variables that are also worth considering, in addition. What's below is a general guide, and not a fixed formula.

Interim CFO

An interim CFO is a person you bring on board to bridge a period of transition. Usually, an interim CFO is a full-time CFO hired for a short or limited duration. Such an arrangement is intended to get you and your company from a specific Point A to a specific Point B.

An interim CFO could also step in while you are searching for a more permanent full-time CFO. Or they may be needed at the beginning of a project and only up until ongoing processes have been established and the internal resources have been trained.

A cultural fit is crucial for an interim CFO, because they will usually be a full-time player in your organization for some set period.

Part-Time CFO

A part-time CFO is a person you bring on board for the long run, but for only a limited number of hours per week or per month. This type of arrangement can vary in complexity. It could be a couple of days per week or as low as a couple of days per month. Part-time CFOs are not intended to bridge a talent or timing gap, but to act as a quarterback for your financial team, and as a confidant to the owner or CEO.

The significance of the candidate's cultural fit with your organization is equally as important with part-time and full-time CFOs as it is with full-time CFOs. This cultural fit is the key to the part-time CFO effectively leading your finance team (be it an internal or external finance team) and providing you with confidence and peace of mind as you focus your attention on CEO responsibilities.

Pricing Considerations for Interim or Part-Time CFOs

Pricing for both interim and part-time CFOs is influenced by the following factors:

- **Are they a W-2 employee or a consultant?** If a consultant, their rate will be higher than you might expect, in order for them to cover for the self-employment taxes that they most likely need to pay, as well as their own business overhead.

- **How long is this engagement?** If it's for longer term, you can often get a discount on the rate, since you would be guaranteeing work for the CFO. In that case, a contract may require significant notice to terminate.

- **Are they in high demand?** The higher the quality of the CFO candidate's proven work, the higher the demand for them and, therefore, the higher their price. Keep in mind that hiring a CFO with a higher value means they should bring that higher value to your organization more quickly than candidates who are not in as high demand.

Sample Interim and Part-Time Prices

Interim or part-time CFOs will cost more *per hour* (sometimes up to two to four times) than full-time internal CFOs, because they, like you, run their own companies. They need to spend some portion of their year in business development to assure a steady income stream.

If the candidate is from an agency, the agency will typically add a mark-up for overhead and profit; the amount of that mark-up will vary according to the agency's reputation and client base.

Let's look at a formula to use to *approximate* a baseline rate – assuming that 1) the candidate is an experienced, independent CFO, 2) the base salary figure is in the range shown in the salaries chart above, 3) and the company brings in more than $50 million in revenues.

Here's the formula:

- Base salary at full-time
- *Divided* by 2,080 (the number of hours in a year)
- *Times* two (to cover self-employment taxes, overhead and benefits equivalent)
- *Times* 90% (guaranteeing work for 90-plus days straight)
- *Equals* approximate baseline rate

And here's an example of using the formula, starting with a base, full-time salary assumption of $225,000: $225,000 / 2,080 = $108/hour x 2 = $216/hour x 90% = $195/hour

Keep in mind that this is a baseline to work from, with a guarantee of 90 days of full-time work. Every negotiation is unique, so apply any discounts or mark-ups or other considerations to the result of using this formula so that you get a figure more tailored to your situation.

* * *

Experienced, reliable financial expertise isn't cheap. But your organization, when it reaches a certain level of complexity, will need experts in several areas to support your core specialty. Finances and accounting, like it or not, is one of those areas.

When you are considering hiring a CFO – of any of the types discussed above – the one thing to make sure of is that any expenditure you make on this critical role should have a concrete payback. Don't let anyone tell you differently about this.

The CFO role should pay for itself.

You'll be glad to know that Nathalie's CFO (me, on a part-time basis) did provide value that more than paid for the cost of that role. Even more importantly for Nathalie, her new story is one of confidence in her numbers, clarity about what drives them, and ownership of an accounting and reporting process that adds value to the business.

Nathalie's transformation came about through the creation of a process that served her as the strategic leader of the business. She knew that there was something wrong with avoiding her company's financial reports, but she also knew that there was something equally wrong with the frustration the process of trying to understand them was bringing.

The goal with this book is the same goal I had with Nathalie: to bring peace of mind and financial confidence to business owners who deserve to rock their accounting the same way they rock the rest of the business essentials.

That was achievable for Nathalie, and it's achievable for you. It only requires a little information you may not already have, and a few tweaks to the process you're already using. If I have done my job with this book, you have found enough tips here to make back your investment in it!

Now that you have a sense of the process, go back to the beginning of the book and start applying the principles one at a time. Step by step, your comfort with and confidence in your company's financial picture will grow.

FURTHER RESOURCES

- *Employee Engagement 2.0,* by Kevin Kruse
- *Small Business Financial Management Kit for Dummies,* by Tage C. and John A. Tracy
- *Accounting for the Numerophobic: A Survival Guide for Small Business Owners,* by Dawn Fotopulos
- *Tandem Leadership,* by Gina Catalano
- QuickBooks – financial software: www.quickbooks.com/smallbusinessquickbooks.intuit.com
- The Priorities Group – CFO services: www.prioritiesgroup.com
- Numbers Done Differently, Amy Bradbury: www.amybradbury.com

ACKNOWLEDGMENTS

I would like to thank the incredible team that has supported me throughout the process of bringing this book to reality. It starts with my family and friends, who sacrificed to give me the space, the time, and the courage to begin, and who gave me encouragement to continue when I faltered (as we always do in new adventures).

My direct family spent hours editing and re-editing, for which you are likely as grateful as I am, as it contributed significantly to the clarity, readability, and flow of my message.

My editor, Grace Kerina, brought her talent, sensitivity, and firm grasp of her trade, which are beautifully balanced in a powerfully professional collaborator. She met me where I was at every step of the process, and pulled from me such wonderful refinements, additions, and deletions, that I felt more and more confident daily in what we were creating. During the time when many authors panic, I became more centered, and she deserves all of the credit for that. I thank her from the bottom of my heart.

Dr. Angela Lauria, Founder and CEO of Difference Press has played so many roles in my journey from having a concept to having a finished product. Listing them would under-represent their incredible meaning and contribution, but I will share the highlights. She plowed, paved, and lit a path through what, for me, was a writing jungle. She identified, routed out, and helped me face all of my own demons that tried to squelch this project before it saw the light of day. She provided the system by which a book was created and edited – all with a speed and quality I hadn't imagined could be possible. It's not often that an accountant acknowledges something magical, but Angela Lauria is magical at her craft. I am honored to call her my coach, and I will be forever grateful for having crossed her path.

To the Morgan James Publishing team: Special thanks to David Hancock, CEO & Founder for believing in me and my message. To my Author Relations Manager, Tiffany Gibson, thanks for making the process seamless and easy. Many more thanks to everyone else, but especially Jim Howard, Bethany Marshall, and Nickcole Watkins.

ABOUT THE AUTHOR

Pam is a one-of-a-kind financial officer, coach, visionary, and leader who brings vibrancy, humanity, and sense of humor to her passion for people, and fun to the workplace. In her extensive career – which has included working with many different types of  companies, from start-ups to Fortune 50 companies – she has transformed organizations during periods of major change, including crisis-level situations, rapid growth, and significant resource constraints.

Pam excels at developing relationships with people at all levels of an organization, creating a culture of engagement, and bringing a sense of relief and confidence to business owners and leaders, as well as to their teams, customers, and suppliers.

Pam earned her MBA and BS degrees from the University of Delaware, and she is a CPA licensed by the Commonwealth of Pennsylvania. Pam is sought after as a public speaker, particularly on issues related to smaller companies.

Website: www.prioritiesgroup.com

Email: pam@prioritiesllc.com

Facebook: www.facebook.com/PrioritiesConsultingLLC

THANK YOU

Congratulations! You have made it through an accounting course!

As a bonus, here's a link to the cash flow forecasting tool introduced in this book. It can be put to immediate use in getting a handle on your cash flow:

http://bit.ly/yourfirstcfo_cashflow

Morgan James
Speakers Group

◢ www.TheMorganJamesSpeakersGroup.com

We connect Morgan James published
authors with live and online events
and audiences who will benefit
from their expertise.

9 781683 505556